Praise for FINDING M

"Neill McKee's work takes us on a true adventure. His keen observations of North Borneo re-imagine a time and place via a unique journey. McKee's writing stirs the imagination and simultaneously explains a place less traveled. His eye and ear for startling detail and understanding of political dimensions make this work a fascinating and eye-opening read."

> —DIANE THIEL, author and professor, University of New Mexico: dianethiel.net

"I love it. It has so many qualities that the usual memoir lacks. Neill McKee is honest about himself, not in any way self-absorbed, but he shares his opinions with attractive openness. McKee is lyrical about the countryside and I felt I was with him as he enjoyed the humorous side of life and the characters in the cramped town of Kota Belud. Nothing drags with different scenes in the short chapters in this book. It is a refreshing journey around a fascinating slice of Borneo with the best of guides."

> —CLYDE SANGER, author and journalist, Ottawa, Canada

"Tracing his time as a Canadian CUSO volunteer teaching in a remote North Borneo village in the late 1960s, Neill McKee exhibits the quality every good story-teller must have to charm readers or listeners: an intense desire to share what he knows. Detailed descriptions provide authenticity that grounds the memoir in a specific reality. As he reminisces about his sojourns in Sabah, he includes the hilarious creation of the North Borneo Frodo Society, which continues in a gentle nostalgic form even today. It is a present reminder that those years he spent in Sabah, Malaysia, changed his life forever."

> —ISABEL HUGGAN, Canadian/international writer of fiction, essays, and poetry: isabelhuggan.com

"McKee's work proves the notion that every journey is undertaken at least as much through the inner world as it is through the outer. From the vast open spaces of Canada to the jungles of Borneo, and from youth through the straits of teaching, traveling, and growing, McKee takes us on a Motorcycle Diaries-type-journey, as written by a man who would become a filmmaker, an expert in international development, and a father. The world that we follow McKee through, almost like ghosts floating over his shoulder, is one of true friends and near misses, one that is familiar and foreign in equal parts. If McKee's first journey was to Borneo, and his second into his own unknown future, we get to take his third journey with him, back into the land of what-was. *Finding Myself in Borneo* is a beautiful book about a brilliant life—a rare read."

—MICHAEL BUCKLEY, short story writer: mikebuckleyauthor.com

"This book is a highly readable flashback to the life of a foreign volunteer teacher in Sabah during the 1960s and 1970s—a time when big changes were just starting to sweep across a land full of eager communities and unspoiled tropical forest. . . . In the closing chapters, McKee makes bittersweet visits back to Sabah. As a filmmaker, he surveys the land by helicopter to find much of what he remembered has gone—vast stretches of forest felled by political and economic forces. Travelers will find this book a fascinating read. McKee's succinct wit offers first-time visitors to Borneo vivid historical bearings to frame their present-day experiences as they travel through this land, still full of many attractions. Malaysians and Sabahans will discover, in McKee's observations, issues to debate on rainy afternoons."

—S. Y. CHIN, Asia-based editor

"*Finding Myself in Borneo* brought back so many warm memories of our own experiences in the US Peace Corps in the late '60s and early '70s. Although we were posted to Liberia, West Africa, McKee's stories induced a lot of discussion about our generation and its ideals. McKee's insights into living in another culture are entertaining, perceptive and informative. We want to read more about his life experiences and are already looking forward to his next book."

—JAMES AND VIVIAN BOWMAN, returned Peace Corps volunteers, Albuquerque, New Mexico, USA

"Neill McKee joins a rare band who dare to write about what they brought to volunteering and, realized later in life, what they received, learned and cherish. The book takes us to the roots of his career when he was a secondary school teacher in Sabah, where he became a filmmaker and then a specialist in media and mobilization for positive social change. That McKee was able to return to Sabah a number of times after his volunteer years, offers the opportunity to match the anecdotes to what in fact happened to the people who touched his life, and he theirs. That is an opportunity and courage I envy."

—CHRISTOPHER SMART, returned CUSO volunteer, Ottawa, Canada

"Neill McKee captures the spirit of Kota Belud, Sabah, Malaysia. As I read, I was instantly transported to the immaculate greens, the deepened shadows of mountains silhouetted against the hot, sapphire skies; the hullabaloo that constituted the heart of the vibrant Asian culture in the era he lived in North Borneo. I felt I was riding with him on his motorbike as the enthralling splendor of the place unfolded. It's an enchanting narrative and I couldn't stop until I had consumed the entire book!"

—NUZHAT SHAHZADI, writer, Fairfax, Virginia, USA

FINDING MYSELF IN BORNEO

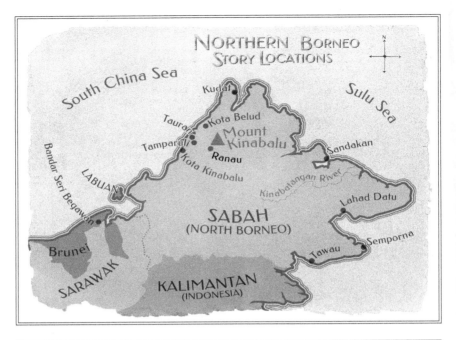

FINDING
MYSELF
IN
BORNEO

Sojourns in Sabah

NEILL McKEE

NBFS CREATIONS
Albuquerque, New Mexico, USA

Finding Myself in Borneo
by Neill McKee

NBFS Creations LLC
Albuquerque, New Mexico, USA
NeillMcKeeAuthor.com

Note: This book is a work of creative nonfiction. Its contents reflect the author's present recollections of experiences spanning several decades. While the stories themselves are true, some events have been compressed to fit in this book and some names and identifying details have been changed out of respect for the privacy of the people involved. The dialogue contained herein has been recreated from memory and is not a word-for-word transcript of conversations that took place.

Literary editor: Pamela Yenser
Book and cover design: Sara DeHaan
Maps: DCNmaps.com | Madison, WI
Photo credits: All photos are by the author or are his property,
except where otherwise credited.

Publisher's Cataloging-in-Publication

Names: McKee, Neill, author.
Title: Finding myself in Borneo: sojourns in Sabah / Neill McKee.
Description: Albuquerque, NM: NBFS Creations, 2019.
Identifiers: ISBN: 978-1-7329457-0-8 (paperback), ISBN: 978-1-7329457-2-2 (ebook)
Subjects: LCSH McKee, Neill—Travel—Borneo. | McKee, Neill—Travel—Sabah
(Malaysia). | Travelers—Biography. | Teachers—Biography. | Borneo—Description
and travel. | Sabah (Malaysia)—Description and travel. | Sabah (Malaysia)—History.
| Sabah (Malaysia)—Social conditions. | Self-realization. | Tolkien, J. R. R.
(John Ronald Reuel), 1892–1973—Appreciation. | Canadian University Service
Overseas. | Documentary films—Production and direction.
| BISAC BIOGRAPHY & AUTOBIOGRAPHY / Adventurers & Explorers
| TRAVEL / Asia / Southeast
Classification: LCC DS597.332 .M45 2018 | DDC 959.8/3/092—dc23

To the memory of Peter Ragan,
who came from San Francisco, my exuberant
"fellow-traveler" and housemate in Sabah.

The world is a book, and those who
do not travel read only one page.
—SAINT AUGUSTINE

The use of traveling is to regulate
imagination with reality, and instead
of thinking of how things may be,
see them as they are.
—SAMUEL JOHNSON

If you really want to know what
Middle-Earth is based on, it's my wonder
and delight in the earth as it is,
particularly the natural earth.
—J. R. R. TOLKIEN

A Kadazan family living in the foothills of Mount Kinabalu

Contents

Acknowledgments

My SINCERE THANKS go to the following people for their reviews and critiques of this book: Professor Diane Thiel, poet, creative nonfiction writer and great teacher; Michael Buckley, short story writer; Isabel Huggan, writer of fiction, essays, and poetry; S. Y. Chin, former colleague and well-known Asia-based editor; Clyde Sanger, author and journalist; and my daughter, Ruth McKee, playwright. My sincere appreciation also goes to my friends: Caitie O'Shea, Peter Hoffman, Nuzhat Shahzadi, Chris Smart, Don Simpson, James and Vivian Bowman, as well as Paul and Evelyn Gervan, for their helpful comments on various versions of the manuscript. I would also like to thank Larry Greenly, writer and editor, for his proofreading and suggestions; and Barbara Daniels for her additional proofreading. I am especially grateful to my wife and lifetime sojourner, artist Elizabeth (Beth) McKee, née Diemer for her reviews and encouragement. Finally, I believe my writing was raised to a higher level through the literary editing services of Pamela Yenser, writer and poet. My love and infinite gratitude to you all for your support and assistance with this book.

—NEILL MCKEE,
Albuquerque, New Mexico, USA

1

Travel Notes: Ontario to Singapore

1.1 *The Canadian* passing through Saskatchewan. PHOTO BY AND COURTESY OF JAMES A. BROWN

JULY 4, 1968: On my last day of work at my father's factory in Elmira, Ontario, Canada, I stood behind its rear wall where I could look down upon the valley and creek flowing past the town's chemical and fertilizer factories. I had a vivid memory of playing in the creek as a kid and coming upon strange mutations—fish with only one bulging eye and frogs with two heads. Were these creatures just imagined? I don't think so. The creek was terribly contaminated. People had few concerns about such issues back then.

Despite this toxic playground, I recall an ideal childhood, a loving family, and—as I grew older—increasing freedom to explore farther and farther from home. I believe my love of travel and discovery started here. While I stood there, I remembered that in the early 1950s, I climbed the pear tree in our backyard, which served as a ladder to the roof of our garage. From that height, I could see a hill to the east, beyond the chemical factory. On that hill, there were large wooden shapes which, in my imagination, looked like elephants, rhinos, and other wild beasts. I had a clear view of what I called "Africa."

As the sun rose in the morning, the figures appeared as dark silhouettes outlined in beads of orange and pink. By midday, I could see the beasts happily grazing on long green and brown grasses that waved in the wind. On rainy days, they were shrouded in mist. But when the clouds cleared and the sun began to set, they would be spotlighted in brilliant gold. On moonlit nights, although a little scary, I would sneak up to our attic to peer out the east window at these wondrous shapes before retreating to the safety of my bed, where they would dance through the night in my dreams, beckoning me to more verdant and sun-filled lands. Little did I know then that I was actually seeing into my future life in Borneo.

July 5, 1968: Finally realizing my childhood dreams. A few months before, as a graduating student at the University of Calgary, I had applied to join Canadian University Service Overseas (CUSO), a non-governmental volunteer organization that recruits people to work for two years in developing countries (Canada's version of Britain's Voluntary Service Overseas [VSO] and the American government's Peace Corps). In April, during my final semester at Calgary, I received an acceptance letter that confirmed I would be going to Asia.

After classes and exams ended, I returned home to Ontario, almost 2,000 miles (3,219 km) away. There, in early June, I received another letter from CUSO that stated I would be posted to a small town, Kota Belud, in the state of Sabah, Malaysia, formerly British North Borneo.

CUSO advised new recruits to keep a diary from the beginning of their adventures, and I began writing notes a few days before my departure. (These words are constructed from those I wrote in 1968, letters home, memories, and more recent reflections on my experiences.) CUSO also provided a reading list, and that's when I drove to the largest library in the nearby City of Kitchener to learn all I could about Borneo and Southeast Asia.

I discovered that Borneo had been divided among three countries: to the north, the Malaysian states of Sabah and Sarawak, and the independent Sultanate of Brunei; to the south, the largest chunk of land (75 percent) making up Indonesia's Kalimantan. On our family's globe, I could see that the equator cuts right through Borneo, ensuring high temperatures and humidity—a perpetual summer for the flora and fauna, and for the human populations living along its coasts and scattered throughout its interior.

I also read that all of Borneo lies south of Asia's dangerous typhoon belt, storms that hit the Philippines, Taiwan, Southern Japan, China's coast, and Vietnam almost every year. At a bookstore, I ordered a recommended title, *Land Below the Wind*, to take with me. The memoir, set in the 1930s during British times, was by an American, Agnes Newton Keith, a colonial officer's wife.[1]

Besides wanting to spend time with my family before departing, I had returned home to Ontario because I needed to earn some money for my upcoming sojourn in Sabah. I chose the easiest means of acquiring some fast cash by working at my father's farm equipment manufacturing company. Elmira was, by then, a town of about 5,000 people with many factories—a beneficiary of the post-war boom. My father and his twin brother were successful businessmen, farm boys who had started from scratch. At the time, they employed over a hundred people at their factory and even more through sales dealerships across Canada and the US. Their achievements were impressive, but a few years earlier, I had made the decision not to join the family business. I wanted to follow a different path.

JULY 8, 1968, MORNING: My notations began again on a Canadian Pacific Railway trans-Canada train, *The Canadian*, which I boarded in Toronto after bidding my parents goodbye. I asked myself, why was I leaving Canada? It was an exciting time. "Trudeaumania" was at its height. Pierre Elliott Trudeau, of mixed French and Scottish descent, had become Canada's 15th Prime Minister—and just in time. Starting back in 1963, the Quebec separatist group, *Front de libération du Québec*, had carried out a series of violent acts, including bombings, kidnappings, and murders. I hoped that Trudeau might be able to persuade Quebec not to separate from the rest of our country.

On the other hand, America's cities were burning. Martin Luther King, Jr. and Robert Kennedy had been assassinated in the past few months. Protesters in the US, Canada, and Europe marched against the Vietnam War. Why was I so attracted to Borneo and Southeast Asia during the time of that horrific conflict? Would Borneo not be just as wild and dangerous for a naïve young man who had never left North America?

At the library, I had looked up the familiar phrase, "The wild men of Borneo," and discovered that the original "wild men" actually refers to two American brothers, Hiram and Barney Davis, who were born in the 1820s and died in the first years of the twentieth century. They only measured about 40 inches tall but could lift heavy weights and beat audience members in wrestling. I learned that they were introduced to P. T. Barnum, the famous entertainer, who put them in the sideshow of his traveling circus, billing them as "The Wild Men of Borneo," a pejorative phrase for the people of the island's densely forested interior. The brothers' handlers and promoters concocted the tale that they had been rescued off the coast of Borneo in a struggle with pirates. However, the truth is that these men were mentally challenged "little people" raised on a farm in Ohio.[2]

A few decades later, the American film, *The Wild Man of Borneo* (1941) would appear. This farcical comedy offensively depicted the natives of Borneo, including a medicine-show con man in leopard suit and "blackface," supposedly a voodoo doctor from the heart of Borneo.[3]

Years before, when I first heard the word "Borneo," it evoked no such crass images of exploitation by carnival barkers or Hollywood moguls. I rather thought of an unknown island somewhere in the southern seas. Through my readings, I discovered that Borneo lies in the heart of maritime Southeast Asia and that it is, after Greenland and New Guinea, the third largest island in the world. I examined a place populated by exotic plants and some of those animals I imagined as a child; a land of diverse peoples with rich cultures, who lived in small cities and towns or in longhouses along wide rivers, where some still sported bold body tattoos and elongated pierced ears. I studied photos of fog-shrouded mountain peaks, fishing villages, coastal rice paddies, beautiful beaches, winding roads leading to inland *kampongs* (villages or communities), and dense rainforests with plenty of vines to swing on.

JULY 8, 1968, MID-AFTERNOON: Our train labored northwest over the rocky shore of Lake Superior and through the Ontario bush. I restlessly passed my time, waiting until we would cross the Canadian Rockies and reach the Pacific Ocean. I saw almost no young people on board, and most of the adults appeared well-dressed and carried fancy hand luggage, which contrasted with my canvas bag. I thought of my cheap metal trunk in the luggage compartment beside their stately Samsonite suitcases.

I put away my large writing pad and tried to be more inconspicuous, jotting down some observations in a small spiral notebook, starting with this strange, gray-haired man across the aisle. He sang to himself, staring into the passing forest and rocks, his lips moving ever so slightly. I assumed he didn't want to disturb anyone, but he also gave me the impression of someone trying to look profound. He seemed a little self-conscious, as if wondering what I thought of him. I felt a sudden urge to tell him it made no difference to me, but we remained in our separate solitudes.

Another man, perhaps in his 50s, wearing a gray suit, drank liquor from a small flask and read a book about US involvement in World War II. Probably a military man, I thought. An American? I wondered if he had a role in that disastrous war in Vietnam.

JULY 9, 1968: As the Manitoba forest turned to prairie, I tried to read the book I had brought along, *Land Below the Wind*. In truth, I found its stories to be about a quaint colonial era. The rasping voice of an old woman sitting across from me frequently interrupted my reading. She seemed to be reciting a series of directions to herself as she gathered her woolen shawl tighter around her shoulders and puckered up dry lips to ask, "Are you going to Regina?" I assumed this Saskatchewan city was her home.

"No ma'am, I'm just passing through. I'm going to the East."

"But we are going west."

"The *Far* East, ma'am."

Again, she insisted that I was headed in the wrong direction.

She pointed to the position of the sun and the hour on the large face of her old wristwatch. She continued giving me advice until, finally, I thanked her and moved to the dining car to avoid further miscommunication. Perhaps I had been reading too many existentialist novels and absurdist plays, but all the passengers appeared to be trapped in individual bubbles. We spoke the same language, but I couldn't really understand them.

Relieved, I sipped coffee. Suddenly, another old woman seated across from me uttered, "God can't see God, we can!" A young woman snickered, but nobody else in the car reacted to this statement. The old woman smiled like an empress dowager, satisfied with herself and her realm, waiting for the next great thought to spring from her lips. I wondered if my relatively young country was going senile before its time. Once again, I buried my face in the book.

JULY 10, 1968: After midnight, we passed through Calgary, where I had finished university two months before. I hadn't attended my graduation ceremony in June because I'd returned to Ontario. I loved my time in this city with its big sky, sun, and view of the Rocky Mountains on the horizon. It contrasted greatly with the University of Western Ontario in London, where I completed my first year. I found that place suffocating—full of fraternities, sororities, and upwardly mobile competition. At the University of Calgary, I had majored in psychology, with a minor in philosophy, but decided not to pursue either field. I thought I would become a clinical psychologist but grew disinterested due to an uninspiring stint as an orderly in a mental hospital the summer before. Besides, it would have taken years of graduate work, and then repaying student loans, and I didn't want to be tied down.

At Calgary, I had joined the drama group, acted in some plays, and taken a scriptwriting course. But drama wasn't a serious

option for me either. I knew I was a wooden actor, and my professor of playwrighting called my pretentious scripts "Presbyterian." I needed a break from studies, not more excursions into
disciplines I might or might not want to pursue. I decided to leave
university with a B.A. Degree in Psychology, rather than waste
more time and money.

I hadn't made much progress on the romantic side either,
probably due to the limits I had imposed on myself. I had dated
the same girl throughout the first three years of high school, but
I always followed my father's advice: "Keep your pecker in your
pants." The thought of getting a girl pregnant petrified me. Who
wanted to be tied down with an early marriage? Young people
found it difficult to access contraceptives in those days.

I had formed a very close relationship with a girl named Ruth
in senior high school. She meant a great deal to me, but we agreed
we shouldn't restrict ourselves—to go our separate ways and see
what happens in the future. I dated a number of girls at university,
but I didn't want to become involved with anyone too seriously.
I wanted freedom to explore the world by myself. And so, I remained a virgin at age 22.

On the other hand, at university, I had started to learn about
other cultures. In fact, the first day I arrived in Calgary, when the
university residence administrator asked me if I had any preference for a roommate, I looked down the list and saw his name
and country of origin: "Wasfi Youssef, Egypt." When we met later
that day, I learned Wasfi was a Ph.D. student in Civil Engineering.

Wasfi was a Copt and very proud of his heritage, one of the
oldest Christian cultures in the world. He spoke English and Arabic. We went for meals together and became good friends. We listened to his 1957 album by a popular female Arabic singer, Fairuz,
titled *An Evening in Beirut*. For the first time, my mind danced
with the sounds and images of the Middle East. Through Wasfi,

I got to know other foreign students from Egypt and around the world.

But that night on *The Canadian*, even with the announcement of Calgary over the PA system, I barely stirred from sleep in my compartment. I had resolved never to look backwards and easily fell asleep again. As we pulled out of Calgary, I woke momentarily, then, once more, my dreams synchronized with the rhythm of the track.

I woke up in the Rockies, gray towers jutting into the clouds all around us. Our train snaked through passages built by thousands of Chinese laborers in the 1880s. Many died in the process. How easy for us to speed through these walls of rock because of their backbreaking and dangerous labor for a dollar a day. I went to the observation car to witness our hurdle over the Continental Divide. After passing through a five-mile tunnel, we began our downward glide towards the Pacific. For a moment, I lost my much-practiced detachment and shivered with excitement.

AUGUST 2, 1968: We were coming to the end of our short CUSO orientation at Fort Camp on the campus of the University of British Columbia (UBC) in Vancouver. We had been engaged in a few weeks of drills on Malay language with an animated teacher, Fauzi Halim. He added fascinating cultural insights. I especially liked the expression *tidak apa*, which literally means "no what" or "it doesn't matter." It's a traditional Malay philosophical statement that life is too short to become hung up on details and time frames.

I learned that a general Malay greeting for neighbors and friends is *datang rumah*—the literal meaning of which is "come to my house." One answer is *sudah makan*, "already eaten." I came to understand that there is no real intention of actually inviting a friend or neighbor to your house by such a greeting, and the answer, while negative, acknowledges the generosity and cultural necessity of offering food, should he or she actually appear.

I also discovered this relaxed attitude in the Malay approach to verb tenses; for example, the simple placement, in front of the present tense, of the word *akan* for the future and *sudah* for the past. Everything else depends on context—no conjugation of verbs, no classification of nouns by gender, and, unlike many Asian languages, no variation in meaning by the tone of pronunciation. To pluralize nouns, you simply had to say them twice, *orang* for "man" and *orang-orang* for "men." Unlike my struggle with French, Malay seemed to be a language I could learn and use immediately.

Returned volunteers gave talks on what to expect. I can only remember Barbara, who offered entertaining anecdotes and wise advice on how to adapt and prosper in Malaysia. Fortunately, she deemphasized trying to save the world, a goal which was never my intention. I just wanted to go to the Far East. Malaysia is predominantly Muslim, and I would have preferred a Buddhist country because I had been reading books on Buddhism throughout my university days. But the more I learned about Malaysia's multi-ethnic, multi-cultural, and religious mix, the more interested I became.

During orientation, I returned to writing some notes on my larger pad. I judged some of the volunteers to be a bit pretentious, holding forth on things about which they probably knew very little, since, I assumed, they had never been to Asia. I mainly listened and asked questions. I observed a group of trainees who laughed and joked a lot. I suspected that they were stoned on marijuana sometimes, but I didn't ask. I had no experience with drugs. I thought of them as kind of crazy but "cool" for taking the chance of being deselected and sent home—the adventure overseas just a lark to them?

Catharine's father

AUGUST 9 AND 10, 1968: My final days in Canada were spent with my high school girlfriend, Ruth. She was volunteering that summer at a First Nation reservation on Vancouver Island. We visited the Japanese garden my uncle, Dr. John Neill, a horticulture professor, had founded on UBC's campus. We drove to an estate in the hills and talked and talked, right where we'd left off the last time we met. We strolled along the beach at sunset and sat by the water's edge. I think I said something dumb, like, "So, I guess we'll get married when I get back if we don't meet someone else." This sounded pompous and unfeeling, but I knew my world was about to change, unpredictably, and hers could too. We'd both seen too many stupid movies in which promises were made before departures and never kept.

AUGUST 11, 1968: We were finally off in the afternoon—a group of sixty or so young Canadians headed for India, Thailand, and Malaysia on Canadian Pacific Airlines. I witnessed the expectant camaraderie as we stood around at Vancouver Airport, waiting to board. I said very little. I remembered the comment I received near the end of orientation, that I seem to keep to myself quite a lot. But I told myself I didn't care what others thought about me. I only wanted to quickly peel away from this continent to a region where, I thought, my life's course might be revealed.

AUGUST 13, 1968: Asia at last appeared through the clouds and displayed itself like chaotic cubes in a modern art painting— Hong Kong's high-rise panorama. Our pilot took aim and dove into this confusion. Suddenly, I felt the thump of the landing gear coming down, and moments later we hit the tarmac hard.

1.2 Hong Kong, my first taste of Asia

We boarded a hotel bus and drove into a world which blasted all my senses: garbage from open-air markets emitting putrid smells; inviting aromas of food and spices cooking in *woks*; braised chickens and ducks hanging in windows; crowds moving in a Stravinsky-like chaotic harmony; and snatches of Cantonese language sounding more like arguments than conversations. Laborers sweated. It must have been over 90 degrees Fahrenheit (32 Celsius).

We checked into a modest, air-conditioned hotel, the Miramar on the Kowloon side, in just enough time to avoid being drenched by a heavy shower—Hong Kong's summer monsoons. Fortunately, I had a room to myself. While waiting for the rain to end, I tried to take a nap. Too excited to sleep, I rested a bit and then decided to go out to explore by myself. As I left the hotel, I breathed in the aftermath of a tropical downpour for the first time—a total cleansing and revival of the city at dusk.

I decided to be brave and take a rickshaw ride by myself, bargaining with a shoeless puller. "How much per hour?"

"Cheap."

"But how much?"

"Fifteen dollar."

"Hong Kong dollars?" I haggled him down to ten. He struggled up a hill as we pulled away. I felt a little guilty, thinking perhaps I should give him an extra tip at the end.

A relieving breeze glanced off the waves of Hong Kong's Victoria Harbor onto my face. I looked across from the Kowloon side to Hong Kong Island, once the center of the infamous opium trade. Chinese junks in the harbor reminded me of an old painting I had seen, minus the tall European sailing ships laden with opium and tea.

My rickshaw puller meandered through narrow streets and alleys to finally emerge at a larger congested concourse. The city had come alive with the glow of Chinese neon signs of every shape, size, and color. Suddenly, I was illiterate.

American soldiers and sailors, on leave from Vietnam, staggered from door to door. The puller obviously had made an assumption about what I was looking for. From the doorways hung dozens of women, all trying to recreate a part in the recent movie, *The World of Suzie Wong.* They beckoned me as I passed. My eyes were drawn to a strikingly tall woman in a tight, cardinal-red dress. Long, flowing black hair; neon shining in her dark eyes—reflections that told me little about her inner life. I wanted to stop and talk to her, but I just smiled and passed by, a mere observer. When I looked back, I saw a sailor approach her, and they disappeared together through a doorway. For a moment, I regretted my aloofness and reserve.

After a stop for a tasty plate of chicken and rice with bits of cucumber, the disappointed puller took me on a roundabout journey back to the Miramar, where I lay on my bed for hours in a jet-lagged daze. Finally, I fell asleep, neon still shining in my mind's eye.

ᆓ

AUGUST 14, 1968: I woke up after a few hours' sleep, ready to explore again. I dressed and went out to walk through the harbor district, passing people sleeping on the streets beside containers of waste. Others busily prepared a vegetable market. An old woman babbled on the stairs beside a shuttered shop. Hundreds of eyes stared at me. A gate opened, swallowing a crowd into the wharf area. Laborers looking for work? I wanted to follow them to find out, but I feared the gate might close behind me.

I entered a quiet street and came upon a host of older people engaged in slow, ballet-like movements in a small, tree-lined park. I wondered if I'd intruded on a religious ritual. Hard to tell. They remained silent, stone-faced, all pretending to fly. In slow, controlled movements, they swooped together, tipping their arms, raising their legs, and extending their heads and bodies as if gravity was not an issue. This, I learned later, was *Tai Chi*, exercise based on a soft form of Chinese martial arts, often practiced in groups, especially by older people in the early morning.

I made it back to my hotel in time to board the bus for Hong Kong Airport with the others in my group. Right before noon, our Cathay Pacific plane took off for Singapore. The experience contrasted pleasantly with Canadian Pacific, especially the graceful Chinese hostesses and the variety of foods served for lunch. I chose Malaysian beef curry with rice and papaya coated with lime juice.

In the early afternoon, we drifted past a coast. The pilot reported we were rounding the tip of South Vietnam at 30,000 feet. Maybe he wanted to assure the passengers that Vietcong firepower couldn't reach us. It was the year of the famous Tet Offensive, which I had been following on TV, when the Viet Cong and North Vietnamese People's Army launched all-out war on South Vietnam, invading Saigon and most provincial towns. The Americans and South Vietnam Army had been caught unprepared and began to wonder if they could ever win this war.

But on that day, Vietnam seemed so peaceful from above—puffy white clouds, bright sunlight, and green jungle camouflaging an ugly reality. I wondered how many Americans and Vietnamese met their deaths during our brief fly past. The dead and wounded could have also included my countrymen. By this time, thousands of Canadian volunteers had joined the US military, and the Australian Army had begun to ramp up its involvement as well.

After lunch, we arrived in Singapore, a somewhat sleepy town, compared to Hong Kong: old colonial buildings amongst sprawling green parks, street after street of two- or three-story Chinese shops, and a fledgling high-rise center. We arrived at another modest hotel, the name of which I never recorded—just glad to have a room to myself again.

I crashed for a couple of hours and woke up in a daze, not knowing where I was. After a shower, I dressed and ventured onto the streets. Outside, a smiling trishaw driver hustled me for a city tour. I built up my courage to ask his hourly rate in Malay, thinking I'd get a better price:

"Berapa harga satu jam?"

He asked where I wanted to go. *"Tuan mahu pergi di mana?"*

I only caught the *pergi mana* part, "go where?" I replied, "Just go around, *jalan-jalan*."

We established a price of five Singapore dollars, about 1.65 USD per hour. He took me into the older part of the city—old shop-houses with orange-tiled roofs, raised covered sidewalks, and open street gutters, which channeled the daily tropical deluge. We entered a side street, where men suddenly surrounded our trishaw, shouting to attract my attention. I quickly understood they were pimps. I saw American soldiers and sailors, mixed with a few Australians, but here the women remained hidden. The trishaw driver had made the same assumption about my purpose as the rickshaw puller in Hong Kong.

My lack of immediate interest left him momentarily perplexed.

Deep furrows appeared on his sweating forehead. Suddenly, his
face lit up. Discreetly pulling a package out of his pouch, he offered me some marijuana. "*Mahu ganja?*"

"*Tidak mahu,*" I looked closely and declined. "*Mahu makan.*"
I indicated I wanted to eat.

He asked me if I wanted to return to my hotel. "*Balik sekarang?*"
I didn't really understand what he was asking but muttered a
phrase I had learned, "*banyak lain,*" very different.

The smile reappeared on his face. With this new purpose, he
pedaled me off in a different direction. For a while, I feared being
driven to a den of thieves. But we eventually ended up at a night-
time food market on a distant street. Bright lights flooded the
area. Loud shouts mixed with Chinese pop music. Garlic, ginger,
coriander, turmeric, cumin, chili peppers, coconut oil, and other
aromas permeated the air. With English, a few words of Malay,
and hand motions, I managed to order a delicious meal from the
vendors: chicken curry and rice, plus pineapple with the skin
and barbs removed in deep spiraling cuts from top to bottom,
and sprinkled with salt. I washed this down with a large bottle
of Tiger beer. People seemed to be happy, helpful, and smiling.

Then I saw her. She was stunning. Our eyes met as she approached my table. She had golden hair, smooth brown skin, and
an excitingly tight blouse. She sat down and began to speak in
pretty good English with a low sexy voice.

"I'm Jackie, what's your name?"

"I'm Neill."

"That's a very strong name."

"Yes, it means 'champion.'"

She shot back, "You want to be my champion?"

"What does that entail?"

As the conversation continued, I came to the realization
that Jackie was a transsexual or transvestite of some sort. It then
dawned on me that my trishaw driver may have taken me to a

"different" kind of place based on my earlier refusals and a mis-understood request.

I found Jackie to be enchanting, a good conversationalist. I bought her a drink. We talked for some time about our countries, cultures, and families. I wanted to know what made her tick. She told me she was a *"Baba* Chinese," a person of mixed Chinese, Malay, and Indian blood. She came from Malacca, the oldest Chinese settlement on the Malayan Peninsula, where a process of assimilation had begun over 500 years ago.

I wasn't shocked or embarrassed by my initial naïveté concerning Jackie. In the drama group I joined at university, I had a few friends who either claimed to be homosexual (we didn't use the term "gay" in those days) or were in the process of trying to figure out their sexual orientation. Because I was a psychology student, they often came to me for counsel. I had no credentials and nothing much to offer them except to listen to their angst. I told them I didn't see their tendencies as abnormal.

After Jackie realized I wasn't up for a more in-depth transaction, she politely bade me goodbye and I stayed to finish my beer. I inspected the kaleidoscope of faces and activities near me: Chinese hawkers shouting out their orders; a tall Sikh in a turban with a shotgun, guarding a nearby jewelry store; a Malay family in flowing, loose gowns taking an evening stroll; Jackie now flirting with an American sailor; and an Indian street peddler selling cigarettes and wrapping some strange nuts and white paste in leaves for people to chew. I later learned that this was betel nut, which gives a slight high when chewed frequently.

I found my trishaw driver and asked him to take me back to the hotel. He drove me through a different area, the Indian sector. Possibly because of my rejection of Jackie, he steered the trishaw up to a red door and motioned for me to get out and enter, saying, *Datang! Masuk!* I didn't resist.

Inside, I met a young Tamil woman with long, slightly curly

hair. Her red and gold sari and her bangles on ankles and wrists softly reflected the subdued light. The air was spiced with burning incense. I followed her and her perfume to a many-pillowed room. The space resonated with chords of classical sitar and *tabla* drums. She allowed me to touch her and helped me undress. Slowly, she unwound her sari and removed her top. Her long hair covered part of her firm and full breasts. We lay together, neither of us in a hurry. I think she knew I was a virgin, for she guided me gently. Finally, I entered and climaxed too soon. She demonstrated grace. I paid and left, a "Presbyterian" no longer.

I had arrived in the East.

2

Lessons in Kota Belud

2.1 Wearing a sarong in front of my bungalow in Kota Belud

THE NEXT DAY, our group dispersed in different directions: Kuala Lumpur, West Malaysia; Kuching, Sarawak; and those of us posted to Sabah boarded a Malaysian Airlines jet bound for its capital, Kota Kinabalu (simply known as KK), located about 900 miles (1,448 km) to the northeast. During British times, they had called the place "Jesselton."

We flew over the shallow South China Sea, the floor of which, geologists had labeled the "Sunda Platform." During the Ice Ages, the low water level provided a bridge from mainland Asia to Borneo[1] for many species, such as rhinos, wild cattle, *sambur*-deer, wild boar, and two anthropoid apes, the gibbon and the famous man of the jungle, the orangutan.[2] I had learned in orientation that the word "orangutan" comes from the Malay words for man, *orang*, and jungle, *hutan*. When the sea level rose, orangutans and other fauna and flora evolved on Borneo into distinct species.

As we glided over the calm sea, I imagined large Chinese junks plying these waters as early as 900 C.E., heading to the mysterious Bornean coast to trade with the natives. We passed Brunei, a small but oil-rich Malay Sultanate, once the seat of an ancient empire that ruled most of the island's coast.[3] Some historians claim that "Borneo" is a corruption of the word "Brunei," while others hold that the name of the island came from Chinese explorers who called the land *Po-ni*,[4] which the Portuguese, the first European visitors, possibly Latinized as "Borneo." (The English sounds "b" and "p" are hard to distinguish in Chinese, and perhaps the Latino sailors added the "o" for flare, as if the island was not exotic enough without it.)

When our group arrived in KK, we hit the midday heat and entered a sweltering, puny airport building. Few facilities in Sabah had air conditioning in the 1960s. By the time we found our luggage and boarded the bus, our shirts and blouses were soaked. We made our way to the student hostel of a government secondary school, where we had to share dorm rooms without ceiling fans. That night, I lay in a sweat under a mosquito net wondering, "What the hell am I doing here?" I tried to write some notes but didn't have the energy. That's when my pitiful attempt at a journal ended.

For the next four or five days, we met with officials who delivered sessions on the cultures, history, and governmental structure of Sabah. I did learn a little about some of the differences in Sabah's Malay dialect, compared to what we were taught in Vancouver, but my mind drifted because I was anxious to get to my post.

About a week later, on a Saturday, I found myself walking hand in hand with Mr. Chan through my new Sabahan home, Kota Belud. I felt a little self-conscious in front of all the townspeople, even though in orientation they told us that males holding hands is only a friendship gesture. Mr. Chan, a short, bespectacled Chinese Malaysian from Penang, wanted to show me around. Mr. Yeoh, also a teacher from West Malaysia, accompanied us. They called me "Mr. Neill," but pronounced my name "nail." By then, I had already been introduced to all the staff. Classes were to start on Monday.

My new colleagues wanted to make sure I felt at home in Kota Belud ("Hill Fort" in English). It's a small settlement near Sabah's West Coast, at about 50 miles (80 km) on the road going north from KK. In Malay, the word for mile is *batu*, which also means "stone." The British had placed white concrete markers with numbers at every mile on main roads, and Malaysians continued this system until they switched to kilometers in 1972.

At the time, the town center consisted of about thirty adjoining shop-houses (called *kedai* in Malay) set on three sides of the square. Chinese Malaysians owned them, mainly Hokkien, Cantonese, Hakka, and Hainanese speakers. The wooden shophouses were painted in drab green, gray, or blue. Some were not painted at all. Gold-lettered nameplates in both Chinese and Roman script decorated the spaces above most of the doors, commemorating the deceased founders—usually a father, grandfather, or great grandfather. My friends explained that the owners and their families slept on the second floor, while their kitchen, bathing, and toilet areas took up the ground floor, at the back.

We inspected the shops' street-level front rooms, crammed full of provisions for sale, some specializing in hardware, some in food, and others in cloth and toiletries. One shop was full of Chinese medicines, including all kinds of roots and tubers, flowers, mushrooms, leaves, bears' bile, and even rhino horn and dried seahorses, ready to be ground into medicinal powder. The front walls of all the shops remained wide open by day. They were equipped with foldable wooden doors and exterior metal gates, which the owners closed at night for protection from thieves and animals.

My colleagues explained that the majority of goods—most very cheap—came from West Malaysia, Singapore, Hong Kong, or Communist China. As I compared the jumbled displays, I could see a huge overlap in inventory and wondered how they all managed to earn a living with such competition. My new friends introduced me to a few Chinese shopkeepers, telling me privately to bargain for everything to bring down the labelled price. They explained that shopkeepers expected customers to haggle over prices, a ritual which builds relationships and provides entertainment.

As we meandered past the shops, I absorbed the aromas of foods and spices mixed with the stench of rotting refuse in open gutters next to the street. I learned from my friends that *belachan*, a paste made of mashed and fermented shrimp, chili, and other spices, was responsible for the most pungent smell. Malaysians love this condiment, along with a variety of chili sauces and *kicap* (pronounced "keechap"), the Malay word for soya sauce. A shopkeeper proudly displayed these bottles on the shelves of a shop we entered.

Mr. Yeoh insisted on enlightening me further: "English 'ketchup' in Malay is *kicap tomato,* but *kicap* originally came from Hokkien, *kê-tsiap*, this fermented fish sauce." He held up a bottle, smiled broadly, and continued the mini-lecture, "Hokkien very clever people. I'm Hokkien, ha, ha, ha."

My friends and I settled in a restaurant, *kedai makan*, in Malay. Large round tables, crowned with white marble, populated the bare concrete floor. Each table held a tray with bottles of some of the sauces I had inspected a few minutes before. This restaurant belonged to Hu Hee Bit, a tall *towkay* (businessman) who, along with his father and his aging grandfather, migrated from Hainan Island off the coast of Southern China in the first part of the twentieth century. The family had escaped war and famine. Hu spoke Malay, some English, and about six Chinese languages besides his native Hainanese. I had already taken out a contract with him for lunch and dinner at about 40 cents US per meal, a choice of a huge variety of Chinese dishes, curries, and even pork chops with fried potatoes and vegetables, Western style.

My fellow teachers wanted to treat me to a drink, so I ordered an Anchor beer while they went for the local version of fresh lemonade, *ayer limau*. Chan explained, "Alcohol drinks make me turn all red and dizzy. Many of us Chinese have this problem."

"Really? That's a pity," I said. But I wondered if that was the real problem. Was it a convenient excuse for not wanting to lose control? Or perhaps they were shy about drinking alcohol because passing community members could see them. I speculated that some parents might frown on alcohol consumption by teachers of their children. But it didn't stop me.

Dark-brown cloth screens on hardwood frames stood in front of the tables against one wall. I asked for an explanation. Yeoh, with his shining gold tooth revealed by a broad smile, answered, "Muslims not supposed to drink. Hiding from Imam, headman, or wife, ha, ha, ha."

My colleagues explained that some local Bajaus, who are Muslim by birth, used these protective screens to shield themselves from community scorn while downing stout, their favorite drink. Also, during the fasting month, *Ramadan*, when Muslims are not supposed to eat or drink from sunup to sundown, these screens hid religious lawbreakers. The Chinese shopkeepers provided a useful service for those who couldn't take the rigors of the rule and for travelers who are not obliged to follow it, according to Muslim custom.

I smiled when I read a metal poster on the wall: "Guinness Stout is Good for You." What could be clearer?

My teacher friends and I cooled ourselves in the mid-afternoon—ceiling fans whirling above. They swished a much-welcomed breeze over our sweating bodies and flapped the pages of a wall calendar featuring a beautiful female movie star from Hong Kong. A few small brown geckos, called *chichaks*, clung to the walls and ceiling, poised to capture unsuspecting insects. I was told these tiny lizards provided periodic approval of customers' statements whenever they made their rapid-fire "chichak" sounds.

We talked about our school, the townspeople, and how Chan and Yeoh missed their more advanced part of Malaysia. We avoided national and state politics, subjects that could quickly take us into racial divisions, and thus should not be discussed in public. Because of the heat and my thirst, I drank a little too quickly but found the buzz pleasant.

As we chatted—an obvious opportunity for my new friends to expand my Malay vocabulary—we looked through the open front wall of the *kedai* towards the town square. This view provided a frame for an ongoing movie on the town's inhabitants. One side of the square offered a view of the *padang*, a field for official ceremonies and sports, including polo. A few small shops on that side were owned or rented by natives, the indigenous peoples, officially called *bumiputera*, Malay for "sons of the soil." My friends told me that they had been constructed in recent years to increase *bumiputera* participation in business. In Kota Belud, the natives are mainly of three ethnic groups—the Bajau and Iranun people, traditionally Muslim fishermen and coastal farmers; and the

Kadazan-Dusun—locally referred to as Kadazan—most of whom farm inland and are mainly Christian or animist in belief.

We watched customers at the open-air market, which dominated the middle of the square. The Bajaus sold seafood and meat, and they also served as butchers because all Muslims require the meat they consume to be slaughtered according to *halal* rules. In Kota Belud, if you wanted to eat pork, you would have to go to Chinese restaurants, or directly purchase pork meat from Chinese or Kadazan farmers. The main meats sold were chicken, goat, beef, or water buffalo—called *kerbau*. Market customers always knew if *kerbau* flesh was available by the sound of steady pounding echoing off shop walls. This treatment made the meat softer and more palatable in curries and quick-fried dishes.

The view from our table provided an endless tableau. We watched a Bajau man ride proudly by on his small horse. He wore a woven black, gold, and red vest with matching pants and head cover; but his brown boots clashed with the rest of his outfit. His stallion pranced along, also in a fancy-dress costume. My friends told me the pair were on their way to a ceremony, probably a wedding.

The Bajaus and Iranun descend from immigrants who began to arrive in North Borneo over a century ago, Malayic Muslims from southwest Philippines—the Sulu Archipelago and Mindanao. Some came from the islands of present-day Indonesia. They first migrated as sea-gypsies, living in small craft as fishermen and traders, along with a few pirates. They settled on the coast to fish, or on the coastal plains to cultivate rice, vegetables, and fruit. They also raised cattle, *kerbau*, goats, and poultry.

My friends explained that Bajaus, Iranun, and Malays, due to an interpretation of Sharia Law, are not allowed to change their religion without permission from the *Yang di-Pertuan Agong*, the Constitutional Monarch of Malaysia. In fact, very few Muslims in Malaysia would even contemplate this. At the time, Sabah had entered a new phase of nationalism and a drive towards Islamization. The Chief Minister, himself, Tun Datu Haji Mustapha bin Datu Harun, was a Suluk-Bajau, so the Bajau center of Kota Belud had become politically important.

Next, a Kadazan farmer wandered into our frame, mounted on the back of his *kerbau*. He displayed two full sacks of newly milled rice, which hung against the sides of his beast. He was shoeless and wore a simple brown shirt over blue trousers, and a floppy cloth hat. A wooden holster containing a long knife, called a *parang*, hung at his side. As a Kadazan, he descended from people who began to arrive in Borneo thousands of years ago. Chan told me that Kadazan and Chinese had intermarried over the centuries, resulting in good-looking offspring.

More drinks arrived as the movie continued. We watched a battered green Land Rover sputter around and around the town square, gathering up customers for the last ride to the capital for the day. "*Pergi KK*," the helper shouted as the driver blasted his horn, scattering suicidal chickens in front of his vehicle. Feral dogs with ulcerated skin and sparse patches of fur clashed over the last scraps of bone and vegetable waste from the market. Three withered women squatted on the ground behind their produce—mangoes, papaya, and jackfruit—displayed on palm leaves, waiting for last-minute customers. Small emaciated cows wandered through the scene, eating garbage and dropping feces everywhere. Goats meandered here and there, munching paper and any other palatable refuse missed by the cows.

I couldn't figure out who owned all these animals and how people kept track of them. With the question on the tip of my tongue, I saw three boys enter the scene. One of them suddenly jumped on the back of a cow while another enticed it with a scrap of paper. The third boy grabbed its tail and pulled without success.

The cow stood firm. The boys retreated and squatted under a tree to talk over their next strategy, while the cow gorged on her paper prize. Throughout this episode, no one except me paid any attention to the boys and their stubborn bovine friend.

A mangy dog entered the shop to retrieve a scrap of food dropped by a customer under one of the tables. Hu, lurking at the front of his *kedai* with a bamboo rod forever ready, swatted this poor canine with such great force that it howled all the way to the foot of a tree in the market square, and lay down to recover. My friends laughed as I shook my head, feeling the dog's pain. This poor scavenger had not yet learned that its garbage collection rights didn't extend into the interior of the *kedai*.

Next, a toothless Bajau man in a plain black *songkok* (an oblong hat worn by some Muslim men) squatted on the raised, covered sidewalk outside. He set up a small charcoal barbeque grill and began taking *satay* orders from customers, both inside and outside of the restaurant. I soon found myself being treated to delicious barbequed skewers of beef and chicken, served with pieces of cucumber and sticky rice baked in woven *pandan* leaf packets. We dipped the *satay* into a chili-spiked peanut sauce as we consumed each morsel. The relationship between the native vendor and the Chinese shop owners seemed mutually beneficial, since *satay* goes well with beer or stout.

We had not quite finished this snack when two strange figures entered our movie. One wore dirty blue shorts, a singlet, and had bare feet. Handwritten Chinese signs of every shape and size decorated his body, hanging from white and brown strings attached to his clothes. Some were tied on sticks taped to his shoulders. A beige metal food plate crowned his head, placed upside down with Chinese characters all around its edge. He stopped frequently to call out phrases in sharp tones, apparently chastising people on the street and in the shops. No one made eye contact with him, and he induced no change of expression on surrounding faces.

This weird figure was trailed by a thin man in a black shirt, dark trousers, and a motley cloth hat. He looked left to right, keeping vigil for his partner. I asked my companions, "Who are these guys?"

They laughed and Yeoh said, "*Orang-orang gila*, crazy men."

"So, what do the signs say?"

"Nonsense," Chan replied, as if this explained everything.

I probed some more and Chan told me he had heard that the sign-bedecked fellow used to be relatively rich but had lost all his money in a business deal. His younger brother acted as a bodyguard of sorts. But Chan didn't know the exact story of their misfortune, and it didn't seem to be important to my friends.

"Harmless," Yeoh added, smiling broadly.

The two figures passed out of sight, still shouting and watching for the invisible threats all around. These strange men brought me back to unpleasant memories of that mental hospital in Ontario where I worked as an orderly for a summer. My job involved confining and restraining patients, helping them take their daily pill regimen, and for the well-behaved, walks on the grounds. I helped to strap some of them down for shock treatments. I came to view these patients, who couldn't cope with the rhythms of ordinary life, as victims of institutionalization. The prospect of knowing exactly what to expect every hour of the day, compared to the outside world, led to a high return rate. Eventually, I grew skeptical of the entire psychiatric protocol.

Kota Belud had no mental hospital and, as I recall, there was only one on the whole of the West Coast of Sabah. The authorities took it for granted that a certain percentage of the population would be *gila* and, so long as they did no harm, the community accepted these people, who were free to roam about and live their lives.

Without warning, a heavy downpour hammered the corrugated metal roofs, interrupting my thoughts. People quickly dashed under the sidewalk shelters to wait it out. But the dogs moved from under trees to open sky, the cool shower a temporary relief from the neverending clouds of flies and fleas, which contributed to their tormenting skin diseases.

The dogs were not the only recipients of this relief. The street gutters filled quickly, washing away the refuse they had collected. Cool, moist air spread inside our *kedai*, bringing with it the fragrance of a derelict world bathed and reborn. The thunder and lightning grew in intensity and then suddenly abated. A steady rain persisted for a few minutes and subsided as quickly as it had begun.

It occurred to me that I had not prepared for rainstorms, but my friends soon fixed that. They took me to a shop to buy a Chinese umbrella—a bamboo frame covered on top with brown, heavily gummed paper. They all laughed as I twirled it in the air. After a bit of bargaining, we settled on a price equivalent to one US dollar. The shopkeeper smiled as he made this sale to the new *Che'gu*, the short-form honorific for *Enche guru*, Mister teacher.

Before we left the town square, Chan and Yeoh took me to the other side to meet the town's unisex hair dresser, Buki, who had a chair in a front corner of one of the shops. Buki not only served both sexes, she was apparently of both sexes, possibly a man who became a woman but not fully. In Malay, they called Buki *setengah-setengah*, a half-half. She had short hair and a round face and wore a bright-red blouse with black pajama-like slacks. Her odd-looking face became attractive when she laughed. Buki's sideline involved telling stories. She was both a local historian and a source of gossip.

Buki asked me if she could cut my hair right away. "*Tuan* Nail, *mahu* haircut *sekarang*?" Sabahans often mix their Malay with English.

"*Bukan Tuan!*" I asked her not to use the formal honorific for "big man." "*Saya che'gu saja.*" I'm only a teacher.

"Teacher good job! You big, handsome man. I'll cut your hair good. Tell you stories. We have fun!"

"If you don't mind, I'll come back for a haircut another day," I said.

After we said goodbye and walked away, I asked my friends a few more questions about Buki, but it soon became evident to me that they didn't think my issues were important. Malay and Chinese are languages that have almost nothing in common except in both there is only one word for "he" and "she." I eventually concluded the dichotomies imposed on the mind by English, and my Western perspective, made it difficult to talk about the complexity of Buki's gender identity. And why did we have to talk about it at all? Buki was just Buki.

We walked up the paved road between the *padang* and the Post Office, passing the tall hill to the left, which hosted the District Office, the District Officer's quarters, an official guest house, and the police station, as well as the District Hospital or *Rumah Sakit* (literally, "house of the sick"), a basic medical facility where services were free to all. Our flip-flops sprayed dirty water onto the backs of our legs, but I was wearing shorts, so no problem, while my friends would have to wash their trousers after this jaunt.

Halfway up the hill, we crossed a steel barrier which the Public Works Department had installed to keep roving cattle and goats from entering the town center. This apparatus of metal pipes with gaps had been designed to deter cloven hooves, but the daily rain had washed earth between the pipes, making it non-functional. Besides, one of the side gates, for people and animals directly

2.2 View from my house, including the so-called cattle barrier

2.3 View from my house of the rice mill and street

2.4   View of Mount Kinabalu from Kota Belud

under their control, always remained open, while the other had been removed. The barrier was the definition of futility.

I decided to accompany my friends on the first part of their mile-long route to the teachers' quarters near our new secondary school. We passed the humming rice mill and walked by some of the more modern houses in the Chinese quarter. We made our way around a bend to a magnificent vista: a wide valley with Mount Kinabalu on the horizon—a darkening silhouette against a pink and orange sky. It towered over forest-covered hills hiding *padi*-laden valleys and bamboo-frame houses with walls made of *attap* wattle and roofs of *attap* leaves, a special palm tree grown for this use. The *kampongs* extended about 20 miles (32 km) to the mountain's base.

I said goodbye to my new friends and headed back to my house to do some lesson preparation and enjoy the cool of the evening. I turned one last time to gaze at the mountain and feel the clean, oxygenated breeze coming from its direction. I thought of my family back in Canada, still breathing the chemical-laden air in our town.

During the first day of orientation in KK, I found out that the Sabah Education Department had switched me to another posting, a predominantly Kadazan town in the interior. From indirect conversations, I gathered that they thought I might not be happy in Kota Belud, which some described as a very "narrow" and "backwards" place with aggressive inhabitants. But before leaving Canada, I had read up on Kota Belud District and its people and had become intrigued. I stuck to my guns.

The first few days after my arrival, it occurred to me that maybe whoever wanted to post me elsewhere had been right. The thought of staying for two years in this place seemed formidable. However, this leisurely afternoon with my new colleagues would prove to be a turning point.

I took a cold shower (my only option) and put on my new brown and blue silk *sarong*, a wraparound cylinder of cloth worn by natives—both men and women. I went to my veranda, a watchtower above Kota Belud Valley, from which I could see the primary school, the town square, make out the beginnings of distant Bajau *kampongs*, and witness multi-colored tropical sunsets.

Gradually, the clanking of vehicles over the faulty cow barrier was replaced by cricket songs, periodically punctuated by the approving cheers of *chichaks* on my inside walls. Distant gongs and drums from a Bajau wedding penetrated the humid evening air. I grew sleepy in my small North Borneo town on the other side of the world, 700 miles southeast of Vietnam, where ignorant armies of the right clashed with those of the left by day and by night.

I was at home.

3

The Rain at Four

3.1, 3.2 Bajau, Kadazan, Sino-Kadazan, and Chinese students of Kota Belud

AFTER TWO WEEKS IN Kota Belud, I still didn't know my students. By then, I'd sorted out some of their first names, but I was sure I was doing a poor job of relating to them. Out of politeness, they said very little, just kept watching the new *che'gu*. As I entered the classrooms, they all fell silent and snapped to their feet, shouting "Good morning, Sir!" I couldn't get them to express themselves or to answer questions. At first, I thought maybe my Canadian accent could be the problem, but I was wrong. I had not yet broken through thick cultural barriers.

Finally, a symbolic breakthrough occurred when, one morning, a student by the name of Datu Tigabelas accompanied me on the mile-long walk from my house to school. In Malay, *Datu* is a term of endearment for boys. It means "prince" and *tigabelas* is Malay for the number 13. He was a Bajau boy of 14 or 15 years of age, the thirteenth child to be born in his family.

Datu asked, "Mr. Nail, what means 'to exist'?"

"It's the same as 'to be.' You know, the mountain is 30 miles over there."

Datu looked puzzled at first, since there is no exact equivalent for "to be" or "is" in Bajau or Malay. He was obviously trying to work it out. But then a playful smile came to his face as he asked, "But how do we know the mountain is over there? We can't touch it."

The conversation continued as we walked. I found it so uplifting that it carried me through the week—Datu Tigabelas, a philosopher in the making.

But my new duties didn't include teaching philosophy; instead, due to a shortage of teachers in the first few months, the headmaster asked me to cover geography, English language and literature, history, physical education, and art. Teaching the Malaysian syllabus, an adapted British system used with variations throughout former colonies, was a challenge. Its breadth of coverage in history and in physical and human geography amazed me. These kids had to study so much more about the world than I had ever learned in school: the main agricultural products of Egypt, the geography and people of China, even the crops and cities of the great plains of North America. In the evenings, I had to work hard at first, so as to appear somewhat knowledgeable in class.

Few of the students could speak or write English very well. I spent hours and hours marking and correcting the grammar, spelling, and logic of their essays. I gradually learned not to ask for too many of those masterpieces. They were deficient in English, partly because they reverted to their own languages— Bajau, Iranun, Kadazan, or Chinese—as soon classes ended. Most walked and talked with those of their own ethnic groups. Using

English amongst themselves outside of school was considered showing off. Malay would suffice as the *lingua franca*.

Not all of the students had so much energy and so many questions as Datu Tigabelas. For instance, Ejin, a Kadazan boy, always looked malnourished and exhausted after the long hike to school, his uniform dirty and damp from fording a river. When he finally reached home in the evening, I expect he had many chores to perform.

Periodically, I would ask him a question such as, "Ejin, what is the capital city of China?" He would wake up from a stupor, rise to his feet and shout, "Egypt, Sir!" This was his standard reply to almost any question, a habit which elicited laughter and smiles from his classmates and the need for diplomacy on my part. The correct answer would follow from the others, such as Jainisah Nurajim, a brilliant Bajau girl; Timbon Lagadan, a quiet but very smart Kadazan boy; or Jenny Chua, a bright and articulate Sino-Kadazan girl who spoke English well.

Goh Eng Kian, a stalwart Sino-Kadazan boy, usually remained silent in solidarity with Ejin, knowing better than I knew the hardships he had to endure to get an education. Goh was the go-to-guy for solving almost any problem or making any arrangement—an entrepreneur in the making. These key personalities could make or break my own feelings about the success of lessons on any given day. The other major factor was climate.

At school, the cool of the mornings would quickly transform into oven-like temperatures by the sun, *matahari*, literally the "eye of the day" in Malay. As my chest began to perspire, my students' faces would turn sleepy. I'd lean forward so my shirt wouldn't stick to my skin and silently pray for a breeze from the louvered windows on two sides. How could I keep them awake and engaged in such heat with so few books and resources?

For the first few weeks, I didn't even have textbooks of my own—an actor on a stage with no props and no prompter. After all, what did I know about world geography and William

Shakespeare, and why was such knowledge important for these children of rice farmers, fishermen, laborers, mechanics, civil servants, and shopkeepers? Given the heat, resources, and logistics, there was no possibility of going on field trips, and we had few teaching aids. We had to make do with my sketches on blackboards, and I never could draw well. Just the same, whatever I drew, my students would dutifully copy.

Our school looked so new and impressive, perched on a plateau of light-brown earth devoid of any greenery. I wrote home to ask if my parents' church and another charity could donate money for library books and teaching equipment. We had no megaphone for assemblies or sports days, no record player or records, no tape recorder, no stencil copier, and only one old typewriter. The money I raised eventually provided all of these things and some reference books as well. This made teaching much easier and more fun.

I also learned to use some of my acting skills to dramatize

3.3 Students with new equipment for the school

and gesture in order to bring more life and humor to my lessons. I had to watch my body language in such demonstrations. Once, I curled the index finger and thumb on my left hand to show the opening of a volcanic crater. When I pointed out the features of this crater with the index finger of my right hand, the class immediately broke into laughter. It took me a few seconds to grasp what the commotion was all about. To them, my hand movements obviously imitated sexual intercourse.

The orderly school assemblies impressed me: lines of students, both boys and girls, standing in their blue and white school uniforms. I recall one of my first public duties in Kota Belud—leading a group of students in a demonstration denouncing the recent claims of the Philippines. Descendants of the Sultan of Sulu, the traditional ruler of the Sulu Archipelago, had protested the entry of Sabah into Malaysia in 1963 (five years before I arrived), claiming that the territory had only been leased, never ceded to the British. A few weeks earlier, the Congress of the Philippines had passed a bill renewing the claim. President Marcos had signed it.

3.4 Kota Belud students demonstrating against the Philippines

District authorities organized our demonstration on behalf of the State government. By bringing in students, they could claim a large crowd had gathered. I could see on their faces that many students didn't really understand why they had to march and stand in the scorching late-morning sun.

I also began to get to know my fellow teachers. We didn't have homerooms, so we would meet in the staff room between classes or during breaks. We changed classrooms rather than having the students shift, and I preferred this because such movement kept me awake in the sticky heat. Besides the two Chinese teachers from West Malaysia, Mr. Chan and Mr. Yeoh, who had taken me around town right after my arrival, there was Miss Harriet, a nervous young Chinese Sabahan lady who tried to teach me Mandarin. She came to my house and giggled a lot into her handkerchief when I made mistakes. Possibly because of all the tonal differences in Chinese words, I could have been uttering curses or sexual expressions. She never told me.

For instance, Harriet taught me that in Mandarin, the meaning unit *ma*, pronounced with a flat tone, means "mother," but when pronounced with a rising tone it means "to bother," and with a falling tone it means "to scold." Furthermore, *ma* means "horse" when pronounced with a first falling and then rising tone, and it can also be used as an interrogative particle when pronounced as a short utterance. I asked Harriet to teach me how to say, "Why should mother bother to scold the horse?" But she just giggled into her handkerchief and suggested we should focus on Chinese characters, explaining that all Chinese languages or dialects pronounce them differently but read them with the same meaning. Although great for China, I thought this was a rather hopeless proposition for me, since there are about fifty thousand characters and learning them wouldn't help with pronouncing the correct tone for any of them. Very quickly, I cancelled these lessons and decided to stick with Malay—a more useful language in Kota Belud and neutral in ethnic terms.

I can still vividly picture Miss Yang, an attractive Chinese Sabahan teacher. I was disappointed when I learned that she was engaged to be married to a man from KK. I got to spend little time with her, only a few exchanges and jokes in the staff room. She escaped Kota Belud every Friday afternoon as soon as classes ended, not to return until late on Sunday. She would generally stick to her quarters when not at school, staying far away from what she thought of as fierce natives with their *parangs* and magic spells. Maybe she also wanted to avoid any in-depth interchange with crazy foreigners.

I have a vague memory of a female Malay language teacher, Miss Zara. She wore loose Muslim gowns. She gave me the impression that she was very religious and that I should keep my distance, but I loved to watch her graceful walk, her small feet in high-heeled sandals darting out from under her long dresses.

One of my strongest memories is of Srikumar Ramanathan. We just called him "Kumar." He came from Southern India and taught science, while also holding the position of deputy headmaster. When I first met him, I had no idea how much he would affect my life and the school. At first, I could barely understand his thick accent.

Anderson, our headmaster from Australia, gave the air of a paternal figure. He spoke in a formal way, distinctly pronouncing each syllable. He would raise his chin high, seemingly looking over the head of anyone he addressed. He kept everyone at a distance. I heard the Chinese community had reservations about his recent conversion to Islam. I never discussed it with him but wondered what he thought I thought about it. I speculated that with my interest in Buddhism, maybe we could have a discussion comparing religions. But for him, talking about such things probably would have demanded unwarranted familiarity.

My idealistic wish to learn more about Buddhism began to fade as I saw how it was practiced in Kota Belud. The Theravada Buddhism of the Chinese community was deeply embedded with the rituals of Taoism and ancestor worship, and I couldn't see how this had anything to do with Buddha's ancient teachings on enlightenment. At any rate, I had a greater interest in Japan's Zen Buddhism, which is based on meditation and intuition. I believed it had much in common with existentialism—a meeting of the East and the West.

There were other foreigners at the school: two young secondary school graduates, Michael and Graham from New Zealand, who were about to finish their one-year term, and two Americans who would become my best friends, Peter Ragan and Caitie O'Shea. The students and some of the more educated townspeople knew our countries of origin, but to them we were all considered "European." The more direct term they used in Malay for all of us was *orang putih*, white man. This term may imply "rich white person," but due to negative colonial experiences, it could also be a somewhat sarcastic insult, something like, "people who think they are better than us," depending on the context of use.

My Peace Corps volunteer friends from San Francisco, Peter and Caitie, had already been in Kota Belud eight months by the time of my arrival. They were well-resourced and had undergone three months of training in Malay language and Malaysia's cultures before they arrived—the US government's thorough way of doing things. My new American friends covered complementary subjects and grades. Peter taught mathematics and sciences. Caitie taught what we called "bridge class," a requirement which prepared kids in English as a second language so they could go on to secondary school. She loved her younger students. Later, she had to take on higher grades for lack of staff, and she also ran the library.

Peter had short brown hair and wore gold-rimmed glasses. He stood over six feet tall, but he wasn't muscular. Even so, he didn't have an ounce of extra fat on his body. He coached the Chinese students in basketball three or four times a week. For some reason, few natives played the sport. Peter told me that his students were surprised to learn that Americans played basketball. They thought the game had been invented in China.

Peter had taken a room with a Chinese family but found the place too noisy, so he moved in with me after the New Zealanders left. Like many young American men at the time, Peter had joined the Peace Corps, partly to reduce his chances of being drafted into the war in Vietnam. Such alternative service wasn't absolute protection from an aggressive draft board; still, he hoped it would keep him at the bottom of the list, even after his Peace Corps stint ended.

Peter could play spontaneous jazz on the piano, and he seemed to drink down languages. He had studied in Germany for a year, where he even took his subject classes in German. He impressed me with his cool demeanor and ability to listen and to talk about

3.5 Peter relaxing in our shared quarters

anything with anyone in English or Malay. Shortly after his arrival in Kota Belud, he won the town's contest in *Bahasa Melayu*, formal Malay, a form of the language that few locals could speak well.

Peter was in perpetual motion. His hands shook with nervous energy. At most meals, he would easily finish two large plates of rice with copious portions of meats and vegetables, quick-fried in rich sauces, and never put on weight. I accused him of "inefficient metabolism"—my joking reference to his mental and physical fire, which burned excess fuel and only cooled down when he slept.

Our bungalow was a light-green building with a corrugated metal roof—a two-bedroom affair with a living room in front and a kitchen in the back. It sat on piles for protection from heavy rains, which would arrive around four o'clock almost every day. It had a washroom containing a *jamban* (a raised squat toilet) and a cold-water shower with a drain on the concrete floor, where we also soaked our clothes in pails, beat them, and rinsed them out. The room also had a water tap on the wall for washing private parts with soap and water, using your left hand, rather than wiping with toilet paper. For this reason, we were taught in orientation never to offer your left hand to anyone in greeting or to touch them with it—a sign of disrespect.

I spent a great deal of time on the veranda at the front of the house, reading, writing, preparing lessons, or watching life in Kota Belud Valley below me. I repaired some of the torn screens on the living room windows so we could retreat there if the mosquitoes grew too aggressive. A DDT spraying program had brought malaria under control in Kota Belud District, but mosquitoes still managed to enter the house, so we'd sleep inside the mosquito nets that hung over our beds. Most nights, I ran my ceiling fan at high speed to catch a cooling breeze.

Sometimes, when we left a door or window open in the evenings, huge flying cicadas and bats invaded our house. The cicadas usually came after heavy rains. They moved like freight helicopters, but we easily brought them down with our broom and then swept them outside. The bats required batting practice. They'd swoop around the room in spite of our warning swipes. We made a game of it. You could only have three unsuccessful swings before handing the broom to the other guy. This would usually go on until the whirling ceiling fan, too fast for the bats' sonic detectors, ended the game. The last one up to bat (so to speak) had to clean up the blood.

On weekends, Peter and I would go down around the corner to Caitie's place, a similar bungalow with a view of Mount Kinabalu. Caitie had an easy, listening way about her and was a good cook, providing a welcome antidote to any tinge of homesickness I felt. We'd talk and read or just listen to Bob Dylan, Joan Baez, Neil Young, Jimi Hendrix, Janis Joplin and the like—our connection with North America's cultural revolution—*Strawberry Fields Forever* and protests against the war in Vietnam. Peter and Caitie had left San Francisco shortly after the 1967 "Summer of Love."

Occasionally, we'd tune in to the shortwave radio broadcasts of the Voice of America, which I thought of as the voice of the CIA. Turning the dial, we'd sometimes come upon some female announcer shouting English phrases in support of Communist China's opposite Cultural Revolution, decrying "American imperialists and their running dogs." Presumably, this included Canadians and Malaysians.

I continued to spend a lot of leisure time at Hu Hee Bit's *kedai makan*. By the time I arrived, Hu was a widower in his 60s. While his family ran the restaurant, he often enjoyed trips to the capital to buy provisions, spend time with friends and relatives, and play *mah-jongg*, a game using Chinese characters etched into small tiles. He also owned a race horse, employed a Bajau jockey, and liked to place bets at the horse races.

Hu was a tall, lean man with some remaining dark hair and an unusual, hooked nose. He was very proud and spoke in absolutes, so I always took what I learned from him with healthy skepticism. Hu liked Peter a lot, while he at first dismissed me as plain ignorant because I couldn't understand much of their conversation in Malay. But I persevered. In fact, I now credit the old *towkay* with a good deal of my Malay language learning, although I avoided copying his Chinese accent.

Hu was the definition of an old fashion capitalist. He never said much about what was happening in China, except that it was "no good." As I got to know him and others in the Chinese community—with their fixation on the price of everything, respect for making money while not showing off their wealth, and their close-knit family connections and clan loyalties—I concluded that the Communist Revolution in China would not last long. Its tenets were the opposite of those of the Chinese culture I observed in Malaysia. Were these overseas Chinese so different from those who remained in China? I very much doubted it.

Hu Hee Bit had a daughter, Rose, five or six years my senior. She helped her father cook and serve. Rose spoke pretty good English and sometimes wore tight and fashionable, "Suzie Wong" dresses with a slit at the side. The rumor I heard, but never discussed with her, was that she had been jilted by a soldier when the British Army was stationed at the nearby base. Some said the soldier made promises, then departed, taking her reputation with him. Local gossip had ensured that her chances of marriage to a Chinese man of her age were minimal.

After Peter left, Rose and I became closer, since her father didn't appear as much in the evenings. I'd usually come late, after general business hours, and we'd talk behind the shuttered doors of the *kedai*. I can still picture her standing at the counter by the cash box and abacus, me at one of the marble tables, her brother nearby, on guard duty against further gossip.

After Caitie left, Rose became my closest female friend in Kota Belud. At that time, I thought about getting more deeply involved with her, but checked myself since I knew I'd regret it. I reasoned that my feelings were due to the general lack of close female company, and she didn't need a repeat of her previous experience with an *orang putih*.

Another local character who became a good friend was Winston, a Malaysian of mixed Asian descent with a striking Sino-Kadazan wife and Asian-fusion family. Besides English and Malay, Winston claimed to speak a few Chinese languages, Kadazan, and Burmese. He was a relatively tall and heavy-set man with pleasant eyes framed by dark-rimmed glasses. He had an infectious laugh and walked with cowboy strides. He claimed to be a Buddhist, but I never saw much evidence of that, for he was one of the most passionate Malaysians I met. From what I'd read, a good Buddhist was supposed to put out all fires of human emotions and desires through daily meditation.

Winston taught bridge class and spoke with a booming voice, making many jokes. He was a dreamer and a gambler, forever on the lookout for someone from whom he might borrow money. He kept on the move in his small, light-blue car, avoiding his creditors and searching for new sources of revenue to feed his risky addiction. I fell into his trap in my first week in Kota Belud, and it took me months to recover my money. Before the school holidays, when I needed travel funds, I staked him out near the government offices on payday and succeeded in my recovery operation.

One evening, Winston's wife came to my door looking for him and his pay. Coming alone to a single man's house was a very unusual thing for a Malaysian woman to do, married or otherwise. Standing on my porch, backlit by moonlight, she looked so lovely. She wore a special dress and extra make-up. Was it only my imagination, or was she looking for more stationary and dependable company? More likely, she and Winston were expected at a social gathering and he was off somewhere gambling. I couldn't tell and didn't probe. I smiled and told her I hadn't seen Winston and didn't know his whereabouts.

In spite of the loan incident, Winston and I remained good friends. He always lent a hand when needed. He knew everyone and everyone knew him. He had migrated from West Malaysia years before and had blended into Kota Belud society. Winston had many stories, such as experiences of World War II, when he was a boy. He, like many Malaysians, had not forgotten nor forgiven the atrocities carried out by Japanese soldiers. "*Orang Japon potong banyak kepala-kepala!*" They cut off many heads in his town.

Winston told me one story of dealing with the Japanese. "We gave them whiskey-*bah*. Plenty whiskey! Those fellows drank a lot, got good and drunk-*bah*. Then we fed them durian, many durians. Those buggers didn't know what happened to them. *Mati bah!* All dead!"

It was a commonly held urban legend that the combination of alcohol and durian is lethal. The myth was probably supported by the ugliness of this Southeast Asian fruit with its hard, prickly spikes on the outside and its edible interior sections which, when ripe, smell much like the inside of a well-used outhouse.

Winston and his wife and children lived in an extended family headed by his in-laws, Mr. and Mrs. Sing. They had an unpainted wooden house raised high up on piles, located across from the Muslim cemetery. Mr. Sing was a stoic character who never said a word to me, just a few grunts. Possibly he wanted to keep me at a distance, guarding his good-looking younger daughters. But the rest of the family welcomed me to drop in to chat at any time on their cool earthen floor, a rustic living space beneath their house where they cooked, ate, and talked all day, retreating upstairs to sleep in the cool of the night.

In a small side room on the ground level, I could also see

Mr. Sing's demented mother. She was chained to her bed to pre-
vent her from wandering onto the busy road. Occasionally, she
squawked like a hen and then fell silent again. This provided the
family with some comic relief, marked by smiles and occasionally
muffled laughter, but no disrespect was meant. In their opinion,
she was only to be fed, toileted, and washed. Nothing more could
be done for her. There were probably no alternatives, no old-age
homes nor other care facilities. I don't think the Sings could have
afforded such assistance even if it had been available. Every family
was expected to look after the older generation as long as necessary and within their means.

This brought back memories of my maternal grandmother,
who became part of our family from my late childhood through
my teenage years. My mother, her youngest child, had to take
her turn in caring for the aged woman. One of her legs had been
amputated because of blood circulation problems, so she scooted
around in a wheel chair. She was a peaceful person of great faith
who neither interfered nor passed uncalled-for judgment on family matters. She remained productive in her hobbies and loved
watching the changing seasons from a sunny corner in our house.
When Grandma was 90, my mother had an unplanned pregnancy
at age 45, and Grandma expressed some worry about where the
new baby would sleep. Then, a month before my mother's due
date, my grandmother left an embroidered leaf incomplete and
went to bed for the last time—a gentle soul who gently departed
that night. As I peered over at Mrs. Sing squawking in her room,
I realized how blessed our family had been.

Then there was Sababacah, a handsome young Malaysian man
of Tamil origin who taught lower grades in our school. His grandparents probably came to Malaya from India to work as laborers
on rubber plantations during British colonial times. In Malaysia,
Tamils remain at the lowest rung of the economic ladder. Their
status is a complete contrast with the Indian Buddhist and Hindu

rulers, missionaries, and traders who colonized Southeast Asia, starting around 200 B.C.E.

I found Sababacah to be great company. We shared the same kind of humor. I became good at bantering with him in a pretend Tamil, a language I found easy to imitate: *"Kali mahganya, kalamakah, ologhamirahingaram, pulagkalaga."* We would argue while drinking beer in one of the town's *kedai-kedai minum* (drinking shops). Sababacah would play along with me in tone, head movements, and innuendo, but with meanings only known to himself. He did teach me one phrase, something like *ohglahoma*, a rather direct way of asking a woman if she wants to make love. (The word was easy to remember since it sounds like a US state.) Bajaus and a few Chinese would gather around to listen to the debates unfold,

3.6 A Bajau wedding near Kota Belud

amazed how this *orang putih* had picked up Tamil so quickly and so proficiently. We never let on that I was just talking nonsense.

Bajau students often invited us to Muslim weddings in their *kampongs*, where the brides and the grooms were required to sit for hours without holding hands, kissing, smiling, or looking at one another, while gongs, drums, flutes, and xylophones provided entertainment. The main feature was the meal, usually fried fish and *rendang*, a spicy, nearly dry coconut-beef curry. The cooks filled the rice with pieces of goat meat and plenty of grease mixed with spices. No alcohol or dancing was permitted at Bajau weddings, and all the guests were required to sit on thin mats on the floors of their small wooden houses.

One time when the villagers saw my foot tapping to the music, they asked me to perform on the gongs. The whole crowd waited for me to make a mistake and, when I made one, they laughed without reserve. Afterwards, they pronounced me *"pandai,"* smart or talented, out of politeness. That night, my ears rang with the sound of gongs and drums until I fell asleep.

My Bajau friends encouraged me to bring my Kodak Brownie

3.7 A Bajau student, Sarimayan, with her family

camera to these weddings so the brides and grooms could get free photos. One time, I arrived late and found my hosts a little upset because some parts of the ceremony had not been documented. They never spoke directly to me about my expected role. I had little money to cover the cost of these photos, but I felt that it wouldn't be right for me to ask them to pay. I was an *orang putih*, so in their minds, I had to be relatively rich.

I also took photos on a visit, arranged by Goh Eng Kian, to a Kadazan student's rugged inland community called "Kampong Melankup." We forded rivers and waded knee-deep in mud, slept on woven grass mats on a bamboo floor, woke around 5:00 a.m. to the crowing of a rooster, and watched the sun rising beside Mount Kinabalu. We bathed in a cool, clear stream and shared a simple breakfast of sugary tea and balls of boiled and mashed tapioca root. Our impoverished hosts were rich with generosity but were so isolated that they knew no Malay. After multiple thanks in Kadazan—*"Poinsikou, Poinsikou"*—we departed.

Sometimes on visits to Kadazan villages, our hosts held parties with plenty of *tapai,* a crude beer fermented from raw rice. We danced like birds gliding through the air on special bamboo floors that bounce up and down to the rhythm of gongs, pipes, flutes, drums, and string instruments. *Tapai* had to be taken with caution, since its alcoholic and bacterial levels were unpredictable and could cause vomiting, diarrhea, severe headaches, and even death. Animists and Catholics held such parties. Over the preceding half-century, many Kadazan villages had their traditions, myths, and most of their *joi de vivre* knocked out of them by Protestant missionaries; although, in retrospect, I have to admit they may have saved many people from death by *tapai.*

A few years later, when I had returned to Canada, I showed a friend my album and she asked me what I missed most about my time in Sabah. Her question stuck with me, and I thought of all the time I had spent on my veranda in the late afternoon.

3.8 Kampong Melankup, in the foothills of Mount Kinabalu

3.9 Posing with my students and villagers at Kampong Melankup

Around four o'clock, rain would patter and then pound on the metal roof of our bungalow, hypnotically drowning out all distractions for a half hour or so. It would end just as quickly, leaving our sleepy town of Kota Belud revived, as Bajau and Kadazan farmers headed home on foot, horse, or *kerbau*. Customers would then resume bartering with Chinese shopkeepers, interrupted briefly by the call to prayer from the loudspeaker on the minaret.

After sunset, I would saunter past the shops, listening to the clatter of abacuses totaling the day's earnings behind closed doors and the clinking of *mah-jongg* tiles in nearby rooms. I would enter through Hu's partially open shop doors for a rice meal and some beer or *ayer limau* to discuss the events of the day. Returning home, carefully avoiding stepping on fresh cow pies, I would go to bed early to ensure I fell deeply asleep before the yelps of feral dogs began as they fornicated under the streetlight on the road below. And I would wake in the morning to a parade of Land Rovers clanking over the ineffective cow barrier, their horns honking the bewildered beasts to and fro.

My daytime schedule would then include a cold shower and a homemade breakfast of French toast and papaya, or a Chinese steamed bun and a cup of rich coffee at Hu's *kedai*; watching streams of students dressed in blue and white on the road to school; attending an obligatory assembly in the already scorching sun; teaching classrooms full of beautiful faces turned towards me with eager ears listening to me expound on things I had just learned myself; discussion and camaraderie with my fellow teachers from everywhere; increasing perspiration and fatigue; a lunch of fried rice or noodle soup mixed with gossip in Malay; another cold shower and a brief siesta, followed by marking papers and preparing lessons on my veranda, while the rice mill buzzed across the road…and then, once more, the rain at four.

4

A Journey through
Middle-Earth

4.1 Keeping watch in my North Borneo Frodo Society garb

Stuck in the queue at a Kota Kinabalu cinema with my sidekick, Peter, and our new friend, Sam, I look around. Under the hazy night lights of the cinema pay-booth, I try to focus on the few familiar faces of Americans, Canadians, Brits, and Sabahans I think I know. The harder I stare, the more some look flat, like black-and-white poster figures in a psychedelic mural. I stop trying so hard, and a few stand out in 3-D—full-flesh, full-color, full-aura dimension. They look so rich and happy, except that one poor woman's face is made out of paper, torn down the middle.

Peter and I aim to make the most of our weekend break from teaching in Kota Belud and pay for our tickets to *Camelot*, a showing in English with Chinese subtitles. I've already seen it some place before; maybe in 1967 when I was a student at the University of Calgary, where I'd signed up to go overseas. Hey, I thought I was familiar with the plot of this lavish musical, but 10 minutes in, I'm simultaneously seeing Richard Harris, the man; Richard Harris, the actor; Arthur, the king; and Arthur, the symbol of all monarchs throughout history. Wow! My perception is so extra-sensual and brilliant!

When Guenevere, played by Vanessa Redgrave, comes on the screen, I have the sensation of being right beside her. I can feel and smell her gorgeous body. I remember that Guenevere met and married King Arthur in the enchanted forest around Camelot. She inspired his Knights of the Roundtable, and later threatened his very kingdom by falling in love with the French knight, Sir Lancelot. But it's pretty hard for me to concentrate on the storyline. I talk to myself: "Didn't that already happen? Is it happening again? Or am I just remembering it happening?" Déjà vu scenes flicker on the screen, running forwards, backwards, sideways, upside down. Too much. I escape to the washroom to take a leak and stare at the blue mosaic tile on the wall, so cooling.

When I return, I only focus on the Chinese subtitles, which seem so elaborate and appear to jump out at me. After a while, I recognize patterns in those dramatic characters—I think I can read them. But I'm jolted back to the action on screen when Sir Lancelot strikes Sir Dinadan, an aggravatingly witty knight. Then, as Lancelot lays his hands on him, all is silent except for the swishing of ceiling fan blades and the constant clicking of hundreds of sets of teeth on toasted watermelon seeds, the Malaysian substitute for popcorn. Time stands still for me until Dinadan miraculously stands up, recovering from the blow. This gives me some new power to turn anything threatening in the film into something positive.

The ending comes too soon and is supremely uplifting, despite Guenevere becoming a nun and England heading into the Dark Ages. Then the highlight: King Arthur knights a boy named Tom—now Sir Thomas of Warwick—with his magic sword "Excalibur" and bids him, "Run home and carry out my orders!" In a flash, I identify with the boy and want to run home immediately, but it's late in the evening and I'm too far from Kota Belud.

The show is over. Peter, Sam, and I step out into the warm city air, which blankets the streetlights, causing a rainbow of colors to vibrate and reflect off the people around us. I feel their warmth. A young woman I know, dressed in pink, is suddenly one of the most mysterious and attractive persons I have ever experienced, both in mind and in body.

It begins to drizzle. For a while, I stare at the drops falling against the illumination from the lights. When I look back, the lady in pink is gone. Had she been there at all? My companions and I begin twirling our Chinese gum-paper umbrellas, spinning water off them. I watch each sparkling drop begin its journey toward what King Arthur called "the great blue motion of the sunlit sea." Leaving the crowd, the three of us meander, spinning our resin-scented umbrellas all the way back to Susan something's house.

EVEN NOW, I CAN replay that experience of October 1968 like it's in the present. Peter and I were staying with Susan, a Peace Corps woman posted to KK. She must have been in another room before we went out to see *Camelot*, when Sam, who was stationed in a town called "Ranau," offered Peter and me some small white pills. The three of us looked at each other, smiled, and swallowed them together. That was my first and only experience with Lysergic acid diethylamide (LSD).

Throughout the rest of the evening, Peter's and Sam's mental states continued to mesh with mine, like three pieces in a complex puzzle, while Susan and a few other guests seemed distant and out of sync. Susan was a friendly woman, but I could feel various controlling motivations behind her words—as if she were transparent. In spite of this, I was attracted to her. As we talked, I was sure I had never spoken so frankly and expressively in my whole life.

Susan and I fried some eggs together—the two of us hovering over the frying pan—and when we sat down to eat them at her wooden dining table, I realized I had never really tasted fried eggs before. After a time, I found myself sitting with some notepaper, working on algebra problems. It was the first time I had done so in over three years. For someone never very good in math, the problems were surprisingly easy to solve.

I had no real idea of time. Sometime later, I transitioned to writing a poem with full concentration, seeing how every single word related to the work as a whole. By 2:00 a.m., I looked around to find that Susan had gone to bed, as had everyone else, including Peter and Sam, who had fallen asleep on foam mattresses on the floor. I went to the sofa, my designated place, and there I lay awake all night long, visualizing my life from childhood to the present.

I got up to the sound of music around 8:00 a.m., still drifting in a state of euphoria. Tears came to my eyes when I heard a Bach cantata on Susan's tape deck. For breakfast, we ate papaya with yogurt and cashews, a combination I had never tasted before. I savored every mouthful.

After breakfast, I went out to take a walk and ended up talking to a British volunteer down the road. He told me he would be leaving Sabah soon and showed me a motorcycle, an old Norton 500, that he had for sale. With a few well-placed words, I talked him into letting me take it on a two-week trial. I could feel his every thought, and I said very little—only enough for him to trust me. If the motorcycle passed my inspection, I told him, I would pay him 150 USD. This was over a month's salary for me, so I'd need to take a loan from Peter and gradually pay him back until I fully owned it. Peter wasn't supposed to own or drive a motorcycle, since it was against Peace Corps policy—too many young smashed heads in the early days of the organization.

A few hours later, Peter and I found ourselves on the Norton, drifting through alluvial rice plains and small villages on the paved road back to Kota Belud. We stopped partway home at our favorite *kedai makan* in Tamparuli for a *kopi susu* (strong coffee with loads of sweetened condensed milk) and *bao* (steamed buns filled with sweet pork and vegetable leftovers, or sometimes sweetened bean paste). They were more delicious than I recalled. We said little, just listening to the loud Chinese banter around us.

Finally, I asked Peter, who was studying Mandarin, "What's it all about?"

"They are arguing over the price of rice."

"Here in Sabah? I thought it was only an issue in China."

"Somewhere, always. You never can tell. Why do you ask?"

"I was just testing your Chinese," I said. "Do you understand Hokkien?"

"No, I was reading the subtitles," Peter joked.

We broke into laughter. Some of the men around us stopped their banter and stared at us. We quickly fell silent again and soon found ourselves back on the road, watching the lowland jungle vines and flowering trees turn to bamboo groves and rubber plantations as we wound uphill. Before long, we descended into a small valley where Kadazans cultivated rice and vegetables, bordered by banana palms, papaya, and *rambutan* trees, which produce a hairy, red, delicious fruit. We ascended once more. As we floated along, I negotiated curves next to steep cliffs overlooking thick jungle carpets in myriad shades of green.

Going around a bend, we saw a Kadazan farmer in front of us on the roadside. Dwarfed by his tapered rattan basket full of tapioca roots, he trudged along like a beast of burden. I noticed his shoeless, enormous feet, which appeared to have been flattened by such labor. As we passed, he smiled and waved at us, apparently accustomed to strange people like us on this busy road.

Peter, seated behind me, suddenly spoke into my ear, "He's a Hobbit!" We both broke out in laughter again. We had been reading the J. R. R. Tolkien trilogy, *The Lord of the Rings*.[1] As the designated driver, it was hard enough to keep my mind on these mountain roads without such additional layers of imagination to distract me. But the seed of an idea had been planted and it would germinate for some weeks. This was even better than *Camelot*.

We didn't reach Kota Belud until after dark. A flat tire had interrupted our progress in the mountains. I had to hitchhike all the way back to Tamparuli to get it fixed while Peter stayed behind to guard the motorcycle and our belongings. That night, I went to bed early, using a blanket for the first time since I had come to Sabah, as the temperature dipped to about 70 degrees Fahrenheit (21 Celsius). Also, for the first time since my arrival, I didn't return to my home country in my dreams. Instead, Peter and I roved around Sabah on our motorcycle.

In the morning, I stood on our veranda, viewing the world in the valley below. Every element of the panoramic scene before me now appeared to be more related and meaningful. But I was wide awake, fully cognizant, and aware of my responsibilities. I had to get back to teaching and then supervising and marking exams.

When I entered the classroom, I immediately sensed a connection with my students in new ways. They asked questions, and my answers flowed like music. I could feel that their search for education aligned with my own new state of mind. My experiment in what many have called "opening the doors of perception" made me particularly attuned to the colors, sounds, tastes, and smells of North Borneo.

My new state became even more evident when I attended the *Tamu Besar*, the "big market," held every Sunday in Kota Belud. People traveled from all over the West Coast to explore the market and to bargain with hundreds of native and Chinese merchants who gathered early in the morning, spreading their wares for sale under the shade of huge trees: household goods, fabrics, clothes, footwear, fresh vegetables and fruit, dried and cooked foods, rice and root crops, spices, traditional medicines, baskets, musical instruments, and other arts and crafts. They displayed these products on raised concrete platforms, in case of sudden rain. Bajau, Iranun, and Kadazan women bantered with customers and one another while constantly chewing betel nut. The Bajaus wore and sold finely woven traditional garments: black, brown, red, green,

4.2 *Tamu Besar*, weekly Sunday market at Kota Belud

4.3 A Bajau woman selling snacks at the *Tamu Besar*

purple, and blue, interwoven with golden threads.

At one side of the market an auctioneer sold cattle, *kerbau,* and goats. The sales proceeded in a way I could never figure out—no loud calling out of proposed prices, just slight head movements by the auctioneer and customers, as if they had all mastered mental telepathy. On the other side, groups of men encircled the cockfighting pit, placing money on the ground to bet on their favorites. Local rules prescribed that no blades were to be fastened to the roosters' legs, so these fights were usually long and bloody, the loser collapsing in exhaustion before being dealt a final blow.

At the *Tamu Besar,* Peter and I ordered our first two *parangs,* long knives engraved with the initials "NBFS." The acronym stood for the North Borneo Frodo Society, an organization we had created after that epiphany on our motorcycle trip home from KK, the weekend we saw *Camelot.* We began to conduct some "research" into the possible links between North Borneo and Middle-Earth. We both liked the character Frodo Baggins, the faithful Hobbit who followed the path of his elder cousin, Bilbo Baggins, by finally delivering "The One Ring" to Mount Doom, thereby saving Middle-Earth from destruction by Sauron and his evil Orcs. We really felt the story was about Frodo finding himself—a true hero's journey.

Viewing Tolkien's map of Middle-Earth[2] beside a physical map of North Borneo, we quickly came to realize that they were one and the same. Indeed, Kota Belud's position seemed to match Rivendell's location, or possibly it was once part of the Shire itself, where Hobbits used to live happily until being driven inland onto the foothills of the Lonely Mountain—which, of course, was none other than Mount Kinabalu! Tolkien's Misty Mountains and Sabah's Crocker Range matched exactly, while his Sea of Rhûn and Borneo's Melian River Valley completely aligned on the maps we consulted. Most of the Shire was, by then, under the South China Sea. But this could be explained with sea level rises during the Ice Ages. The underwater topographical maps we inspected showed Tolkien's river beds and mountains, which had been buried under salt water. (*See next page.*)

In the months that followed, we sped up the frequency of our fantasy meetings, sending out the minutes far and wide and thereby increasing membership. We claimed many discoveries. As one of two Founding Fathers and the Corresponding Secretary of the NBFS, I had worldwide exchanges with organizations and newsletters. The list included The British Fantasy Society, *The Sprung Blah* by the Speculative Fiction Club of Aviano, Italy, and some other groups that had appropriated Tolkien names—*Anduril, Mathom, Caer Pedryvan, Thain Peregrin*—as well as The Tolkien Society of London, itself.

Caitie created our letterhead in Elvish and helped write many

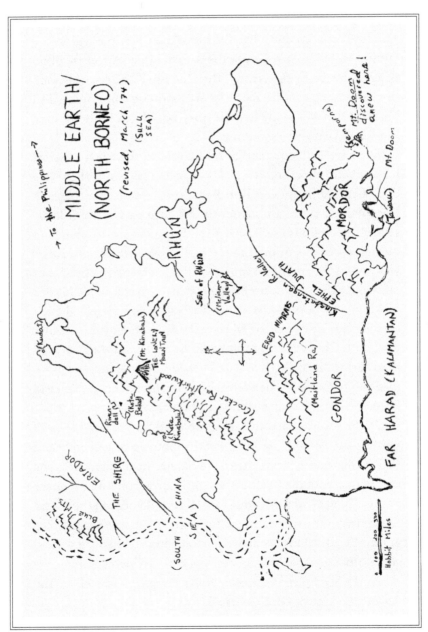

4.4 Map of correlation between North Borneo and Middle-Earth

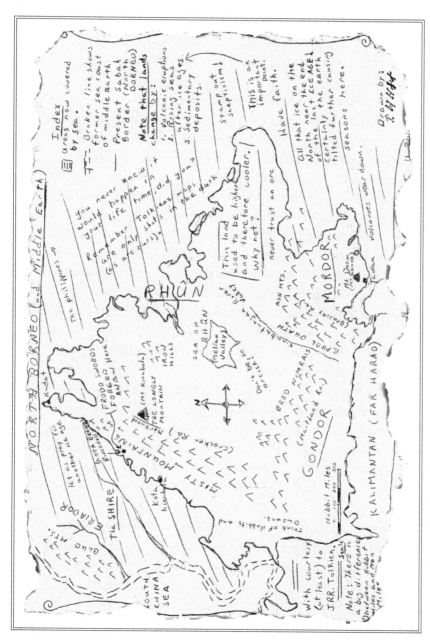

4.5 Annotated map of North Borneo/Middle-Earth

words in Tolkien's runes. She also contributed stories to our newsletter and cheered us on. I honestly can't remember where all our fervor took us, but I recall how very diligently we pursued our goal.

We ordered membership cards from a Chinese printer in KK and offered them in our newsletters: "Please write us and enclose one US dollar if you want to join and possess your own Elvish-script membership card. (All funds to be used for further research and publication of findings.) Then, if you are satisfied, you may even want an Elvish-script sword forged here in Kota Belud (probably Rivendell), near the Lonely Mountain, by a native who has forgotten the script of old, but who is being instructed by us for his benefit in making a living. You can become an active member and publish our research if you really want to. We are not trying to hide anything, just write us and see."

We asked people to have faith in our discoveries. I sold myself as one who was "blindly pursuing the truth of the ages, through Tolkien nights in transcendental stages." Peter added this to his photo: "Battered though his appearance be, in him there lies a subtlety that none but he who is true to the cause can perceive."

During the rest of 1968 and 1969, we received requests from California (of course), other US states, the United Kingdom, Canada, Germany, France, Italy, New Zealand, Australia, the Philippines, and East and West Malaysia. We were surprised by the excitement we had stirred, which incredibly mirrored our own enthusiasm.

Steven Farnum of Berkeley, California wrote, "The name of your Society started my imagination running. To stop it, I had to write you and ask you about what it is like and how it works (and so forth). Any society who uses the slogan, 'In Frodo We Trust, In Orcs We Disgust,' must be a good one."

James Brown of Santa Clara, California wrote, "Dear Sirs, Yes, please rush my membership card to the above address. I understand that this entitles me to one year's free subscription to the *Hobbit Gazette* and that I am under no obligation to buy a Hobbit button unless I freely choose to do so."

Anne Etkin of Riverdale, Maryland got the point. In her second letter, she wrote:

Dear Frodoians,

Thank you for the card and map of North Borneo as Middle-Earth. What a delight to be a member of the NBFS! I had no idea of the remarkable cartographic coincidence. I exclaimed aloud "Orcs!" on reading of your discoveries being validated by Margaret Mead's earlier research. This led my husband to inquire about my health. I haven't, as of yet, heard whether I have incurred obligations along with the card. I wonder, wistfully, if maybe the NBFS doesn't do anything. Pleasant thought, just to be. However, I'm sure that if it does anything that anything will suit me, and it will be pleasantly improbable.

Ode Ulvear from somewhere sent a less-typical second letter with her check for one US dollar:

Dear Friend of Frodo,

Thank you for your interesting response to my letter. I am delighted with your offer of Artist in Residence. Thank you very much and I do accept. My-My, this is exciting. At this late point in my life I could use something fresh to get my old body in gear. I was 95 on my last birthday. That was May 20, 1874. I'm a Taurian with my moon in gimini [sic] and of course my ruling planet is Venus. Well, please write to me again and let me know how I might get myself to those Hobbits.

Any small doubts we had harbored about our claims were assuaged when, one day, I read to Peter an interesting article from

Wangsa News Service in *The Sabah Times*:

Wednesday March 12, 1969:

'Oily Man' Scare hits Kota Belud—Rumours about an
Orang Minyak (Oily Man) is [sic] circulating here like a wild
fire. Villagers, coming home from late outings, claim to have
seen him. The origin of the rumours is not known, but it is
creatin [sic] a scare among Kota Belud residents, especially
the women folk. A married man said he heard a few nights
ago a distant cry—like that of a friend, calling out his name.
He called out thrice but received no reply. Remembering the
rumours, he took fright and went back into the house and
locked the door. However, nothing eventful happened that
night. Many superstitious housewives are scared and some do
not want to go out at night. One very frightened housewife
went so far as to spend the night with her neighbours when
her husband did not return early.[3]

I looked at Peter and our eyes met and widened. We both shouted,
"Gollum!"

This is the name of an important character introduced in Tolkien's earlier book, *The Hobbit*. He is a slimy "River-folk" who
possessed the magic Ring for some time. It prolongs his life, but
he becomes very secretive and possessive, until it consumes him.
The newspaper account matched our readings of the evil nature
of Gollum, and we knew then and there our creation of the NBFS
was not in vain. Tolkien's story has him burning up with "The
One Ring" when he fell into Mount Doom. But did Gollum really
perish?

NBFS member D. V. Jenkins, a geologist then based in Kota
Kinabalu, provided further clues in a letter which led me to a
whole new line of enquiry through reading the texts of historical explorations of North Borneo, published in 1922. I found a
reference in that book to a 1910 exploration of Mount Kinabalu,
where it was mentioned that the local natives believed the summit

was guarded by a fierce dragon. The monster had caused the death of many Chinese explorers.

The story is about a Chinese man by the name of Po Kong who fell in love with the daughter of a Kadazan-Dusun chief. Her name is not mentioned in the tale. The chief opposed the marriage because the girl was already engaged to a man of her own race, but the young couple eloped. After wandering about, they found themselves on the summit of Mount Kinabalu. There, in the evening, they saw a strange light and recognized it was coming from a dragon outside his cave, alternatively swallowing and spitting out an enormous carbuncle of brilliant luster. Po Kong and his wife gathered two handfuls of mud. They waited for the next time the jewel was on the ground and then threw the mud straight at the dragon's eyes. Po Kong seized the jewel and wrapped it in his coat. Suddenly, all turned dark as Po Kong leapt over a deep gorge with the jewel, leaving his wife behind. The blinded dragon fell into the chasm and was killed. Unfortunately, Po Kong never went back to find his wife. Eventually he came to Saiap Village in Tempasuk District, where he settled and spent the rest of his days making enormous jars, some of which may still be seen today.[4]

Although we had no proof, our thoughts brought us to the possibility that Tolkien may have been inspired by such a mythological account. Perhaps the tale had influence on Tolkien's creation of the "Lonely Mountain," guarded by Smaug the dragon in *The Hobbit*.[5] Thorin and his company of dwarves, along with Hobbit Bilbo Baggins, disturbed his peace. Then, later, the bowman, Bard of Esgaroth, killed the beast.[6] We speculated that Tolkien had journeyed to North Borneo or read about its early exploration. How could he have dreamed up his story otherwise?

We wrote to Tolkien's publisher, George Allen & Unwin Ltd., in London, wondering if we would ever receive a reply. Who were we but lowly first readers on a faraway tropical island?

Our letter took a long time to reach the right hands, but finally and much to our surprise, Miss J. Hill, Press Officer at George

Allen & Unwin, wrote back in a letter dated 20th November 1969: "I am sure that Professor Tolkien will be delighted to know that you have formed a North Borneo Frodo Society. Professor Tolkien is busily writing the prequel to *The Lord of the Rings* at the moment and is answering very few letters himself, and so what I propose to do is to take your letter to him when I visit him within the next few weeks."

Our correspondence led to the most delightful request of all, from a David J. Varley, Export Manager for the publisher. The final sentence was underlined to emphasize its importance: "Could you also send a membership card to Professor Tolkien himself, I am sure he would much treasure it."

I must flash forward here, regarding how the NBFS continued to spread throughout the twentieth century. In the July 25, 1973 issue of *Punch*, a popular British satirical magazine, writer Jonathan Sale wrote in an article titled *Ring Three Times* that Tolkien "societies have been springing up everywhere, the most improbable being the Frodo Society of North Borneo."[7]

In 1974, Stuart Clark, Editor at The Tolkien Society of London, ended a letter to us with these immensely satisfying words, underlining the most important: "I write to you as you are definitely among the leading Societies in the world today, as, with ourselves, you are the second Society to be honoured with official patronage from JRRT himself. I look forward to hearing from you. Elen Sila Lumann' Omentielvo!!"

The great Professor Tolkien, who had sparked our imaginations, died in 1973, but his legacy and fame—and our Society—lives on. We were honored to be mentioned in J. R. R. Tolkien's authorized biography by Humphrey Carpenter, published in 1977: "The wildfire of this American enthusiasm spread to other countries. At festivities in Saigon, a Vietnam dancer was seen bearing the lidless eye of Sauron on his shield, and in North Borneo a 'Frodo Society' was formed."[8]

Although I had made many moves since the NBFS's creation,

a letter dated the 18th of September 2000, from Ricardo Lopez and Ana Correa of Lisbon, Portugal, managed to reach me with these words of great importance:

> We are, respectively, a biologist and an architect. This year we spent our vacation in Malaysia and visited Mount Kinabalu Park in Sabah. We heard about the North Borneo Frodo Society and your claim that Sabah is in fact Tolkien's Middle-Earth, but we were still amazed at what we found. It really is Middle-Earth! We were always waiting for a Hobbit to come out of a tree! Because we fell deeply in love with Mount Kinabalu, and we both loved *The Lord of the Rings*, we would like very much to become members of the North Borneo Frodo Society. We'll be waiting to hear from you soon. Best Regards.

Back in 1968 and early 1969, all these discoveries and the NBFS's international recognition were far in the future. In fact, when we first came up with the idea of the NBFS, due to heavy teaching duties I had to put off further research on the importance of Mount Kinabalu until I had a chance to climb it. I could hardly wait for the opportunity.

In keeping with my new identity as a Founding Father of the NBFS, I painted my motorcycle helmet black, with my name on the front in silver Elvish script. Very few Sabahans asked what the writing meant, but if they did I would say, "It means 'Neill' in an ancient language." I didn't want them to think I was *gila* like the Chinese guy who visited Kota Belud's town square almost every day, with all the signs hanging from him. Fortunately, the townsfolk never probed further about my helmet.

I sometimes brought my NBFS *parang* with me on motorcycle trips but avoided public display, not wanting to be responsible for inciting any form of violence. Occasionally, I offered rides to farmers and their *barang* (goods or belongings), especially when I encountered them in the middle of nowhere.

One day when I was returning from a visit with Sam in Ranau, coming down the road under construction in the rain, I saw a heavily laden Kadazan farmer with very large (and possibly hairy) bare feet slipping along the side. I was sporting my dark green army-surplus poncho, sunglasses, and my Elvish-script helmet. I pulled up beside him to ask, *"Pergi mana?"* Where are you going? This is a polite way of saying "hello" in Sabah, the answer to which is *"Disana!"* or *"Disaaana!"* or *"Disaaaana!"* This means "over there," the length of the drawn-out extra vowels and degree of forward thrust of the chin indicating approximate distance, without providing specificity on exact destination, which is neither required nor expected.

At any rate, this man took one look at me and an expression of horror came over his face. He seemed to turn almost white, something I had never seen a Kadazan face do before. Then he leapt up and over the red clay embankment alongside the road. I quickly parked my motorcycle and climbed up the bank to see if he was OK. I peered over and spotted him slipping down a steep slope towards the jungle. I yelled out, *"Saya mahu membantu saja!"* (I only want to help you.) This just increased his state of terror, and he slipped further downward in a wild effort to escape the *hantu* (the Malay word for spirit or ghost), who had suddenly appeared before him on the road. There was nothing more I could do.

As I continued my slow journey, occasionally stopping to clear the sticky clay from my motorcycle wheels, I made a resolution to be more careful of others walking alongside roads, especially in the *ulu*—the backwoods. Still, I rationalized, he would probably recover and reach home safely, and I had provided him with an incident that would spur an excellent ghost story, one which would live on in these parts for many years to come.

After all, Tolkien's Hobbits, Frodo and Bilbo, loved such stories and recounted them endlessly.

5

Bonding with Borneo

5.1 On the summit of Mount Kinabalu

THE MALAY ADJECTIVE Sabahans used for Kota Belud in the
1960s was *sempit,* which means "narrow" physically or "confining" and "dull" in a psychological sense. When I arrived in Kota
Belud, I was so quickly thrown into teaching and meeting new
people that I didn't feel this narrowness at first. But after some
time, I learned that Kota Belud was, in its own way, like any small
town in North America, such as the one I grew up in. Your every
word and movement could be watched, recorded, and reported
through gossip. I knew that periodic escapes were essential to

5.2 Heading to Mantanani Island in the South China Sea

me. They helped me learn more about myself and how to bond with Borneo.

During the first few months, I got out of town on weekends by joining in explorations with my male students. Female students couldn't come, since it would have been totally against community norms for them to mix with boys and male teachers on such excursions. Girls' reputations and future prospects, including chances of marriage, would be at stake. Besides, they usually had domestic duties to perform when not in school.

On one occasion, I joined Goh Eng Kian and some other students taking a Land Rover to Kuala Abai, a fishing village on the South China Sea. We boarded a small motorboat for Mantanani Island and hiked through the jungle to a pristine beach on the northern side. We picnicked on too much spicy food, buried ourselves in sand, and avoided sharks while diving in a coral reef. The

5.3 Students playing on the beach at Mantanani Island

boys talked about the danger of pirates, who had infested these waters for many centuries—even though, at the time, kidnapping for ransom was not yet in fashion.

My students often discussed Mat Salleh, a Suluk-Bajau outlaw who rebelled against the British, a "Robin Hood" of North Borneo by some accounts. Legend has it that he fought against unfair taxes imposed by local elites on behalf of the British North Borneo Company. In his day, he had many followers among the Bajau, Suluk, and Kadazan communities. Cunning and fast moving, he set up forts and hideouts in many places, including Kota Belud, to evade the colonial police. Finally, in 1900, the police shot him in the head while he peered over the wall of his fort in Tambunan, a small community in the interior. His followers carried on the rebellion for five more years before they surrendered.

There's a legend that the name, "Mat Salleh," actually comes from encounters the natives of Borneo had with drunken Western sailors. When sober Europeans called these characters "mad sailors," locals heard "mat salleh," and the term has since been used to label unruly people, like the famous outlaw. (I told Peter and Caitie my secret NBFS name was *Mat Paku bin Kunci*, which means "Mad Nail son of Key" in Malay, and they had to agree.)

One Saturday, Goh Eng Kian and others organized a hike over the embankments of *padi* fields and through Kadazan villages where people scattered, possibly thinking we were Filipino invaders. We scaled a high hill on the southwest side of town, climbing around hill-*padi*, which Kadazans cultivate on slopes using slash-and-burn methods. We carefully worked our way through razor-sharp blades of tall *lalang* grass, which can cut any exposed skin. Each time we reached the top of one slope, puffing and sweating profusely, there was another one to conquer.

At first, the students tried to help me, concerned when I slipped a little. "Mr. Nail, you OK?" Goh called out, "I can pull you up."

"I'm fine, Goh. I just failed the grade, but I will rise again."

I wondered whether they thought I'd lived a sheltered life in Canada during my childhood and teens. Gradually, they let me do my own thing, and I became part of the team, at least for the day. In Malaysia, it's hard for students not to treat their teachers with great deference, and I didn't want to upset this *status quo* too much because it could have had repercussions on our relationships in class.

After a couple of hours and many bottles of water, we finally arrived at the top to view Kota Belud Valley laid out before us, the South China Sea beyond, and Mount Kinabalu beckoning on the other side. We rested on dry earth and resumed our banter.

"Did Mat Salleh climb this hill?" Dahulim asked.

"Do you feel his *hantu*?" Eng Kian retorted.

Hantu-hantu (ghosts) were a continual topic of conversation, and I had become tuned into their humor enough to throw in my two bits. "I have seen a *hantu* in a glowing white form on this hill at night. It's visible from my veranda."

"Mr. Nail, are you sure you were not drinking *tapai*?" Eng Kian asked.

"No *tapai*. I'm sure Mat Salleh's *hantu* inhabits this hill," I insisted. "I can feel him now."

"Mr. Nail, how can you prove it? What are your scientific observations and proof?" Awang asked.

"I teach literature, not science, Awang. Literature demands different kinds of observations and no proof."

After a late picnic lunch consisting of tins of small curried sardines and tasty sticky rice served in packets of woven *pandan* leaf strands, with jackfruit and pineapple for dessert, it began to rain. We had rested too long.

We descended via a steeper and faster route through thick jungle, holding onto vines to keep from slipping, our bums sliding on the trail. Finally, we arrived at a small rubber tree plantation. The canopy provided some protection from the rain. We washed ourselves in a cool creek and applied salt to the leeches which had hitchhiked on our bodies. Some students tried to burn them off with matches, a precarious business.

The rain ceased as we reached the road at dusk. Soon, a truck arrived to take us back to town—Goh's meticulous arrangements and timing. As we flew down the road, I stood, catching the breeze to dry my itchy crotch, thinking only of the cooling shower and talcum powder awaiting me at home.

For me, climbing this high hill was practice for the ultimate bond with North Borneo, the ascent of Mount Kinabalu, the highest mountain in Southeast Asia. It rises 13,435 feet (4,095 meters) above sea level, a lonely granite outcrop in the jungle. It's one of the youngest non-volcanic mountains in the world.

After reading about it myself, I taught my students that it's an

5.4 View of Mount Kinabalu's summit

"igneous intrusion" formed within the last 10,000,000 years when molten rock, trapped beneath the surface of the earth, pushed the hard rock above into a dome. Its summit was then shaped and smoothed into a sloping plateau by daily wind and rain throughout the ages. Today, the mountain is said to be still rising at a rate of about five millimeters per year.

Beginning in colonial times, expatriates rose to the challenge of climbing Mount Kinabalu. In 1851 and again in 1858, Sir Hugh Low attempted to climb the mountain with Kadazan-Dusun porters. They reached the summit plateau but never reached the highest peak. As recorded by the British in 1888, that honor was left to John Whitehead and some daring Kadazan-Dusun porters.

However, the mythological history of ascending the famed mountain reaches much further back in time. Another common variation of the Kinabalu dragon myth holds that the mountain's name comes from *China Balu,* which means "Chinese widow" in Malay or Kadazan-Dusun. According to this legend, a Chinese prince ascended the mountain in search of a huge pearl guarded by a ferocious dragon. He had to prove his prowess to marry a Kadazan-Dusun woman. But for some unknown reason, he abandoned her and returned to China. With a broken heart, the woman went to the mountain's summit to mourn, where her spirit remains to this day.

During my research for the NBFS, I found that this popular version was disputed from colonial times. A more plausible explanation, written by a Catholic missionary in the early part of the twentieth century, was that the derivation of the name of the mountain is completely native, nothing to do with the mythical Chinese visitors. He claimed that in Kadazan-Dusun, *ki* means "there is," *na* is a prefix denoting action, and *bahu* or *balu* (in Kadazan-Dusun, the letters "h" and "l" are interchangeable) refers to a small house where people's corpses are placed before burial. Hence, "Kinabalu," or "there is a place where the dead go."[1]

One Kadazan-Dusun creation myth features a huge rock (Mount Kinabalu) thrust down to earth by the god Kinohiringan and his wife Umunsumunda, to form the land and sea into a reflection of the beauty of heaven. While Umunsumunda shaped the earth, Kinohiringan created the sky, clouds, and everything above the earth. This myth includes an eagle called "Kondiu," a magnificent bird who reported on the beauty of their creation, but also brought bad news that shook Kinohiringan's pride. The cloud was too small for the size of the earth below it, so Umunsumunda recreated the earth to match the size of the clouds, setting Mount Kinabalu as the center of the world and restoring her husband's pride.[2]

This reference to a powerful and helpful eagle provided even more evidence of the similarities between Kadazan myths and the stories in *The Lord of the Rings*, in which eagles act as spies for Hobbits and their allies—looking out for Orcs, guarding strategic high places, carrying messages, and even transporting our heroes to important battles.

Mount Kinabalu is famous for more than myths. It is home to one of the most diverse congregations of fauna and flora in the world, from the tropical rain forest below, to the temperate world above. As you ascend, the trees decrease in height but not in beauty. They look like purposely shaped gardens of Japanese *bonsai*. Many of the plant and animal species on Kinabalu cannot be found elsewhere in the world. On its slopes are hundreds of kinds of orchids and dozens of types of rhododendrons; the world's largest and rarest of pitcher plants; and numerous bamboo species, mosses, oak trees, fig trees, and ferns. Living among the plants are over five hundred bird species, notably the Red-breasted Tree Partridge and the Crimson-headed Wood Partridge. Also endemic to Mount Kinabalu are many species of reptiles; spiders, moths, butterflies, and other insects; small mammals such as the Kinabalu Shrew, the Kinabalu Ferret, and Thomas's Flying Squirrel; and unusual species such as the Kinabalu Giant Red Leech, which is capable of devouring the Kinabalu Giant Earthworm.

When we climbed the trail up the mountain in April of 1969, it had already been well-developed, marked, and protected, but we still were required to be accompanied by a Kinabalu Park guide. Also joining us were a Peace Corps friend, Tom; my dueling buddy in pretend Tamil, Sababacah; and Mr. Yeoh, who wasn't in the best of shape but provided commentary on the whole process.

Yeoh would stop halfway up a slope and say things like, "Mr. Nail, why you want me to climb this mountain? You think I'm stupid?"

"No, Yeoh, mountains are just meant for climbing."

"Chinese saying, 'Men don't trip on mountains, they stumble on stones.'"

"Yeoh, you always seem to be stoned. Don't stumble."

Such banter would go on until Tom would cry, "Stop, stop! I'll fall off this cliff!"

Tom came from Minnesota. He taught primary school in the small Kadazan village of Tenghilan, an isolated place on the road between Kota Belud and KK. Tom was fluent in Malay and could also speak some Kadazan. Almost any words in English seemed to freak him out, since he seldom had a chance to speak it at his post. He even dreamed in his new languages. I figured he needed periodic infusions of English to bring him back to reality. Tom agreed it was good for him, but he seemed to cringe at our words, a kind of culture shock in reverse.

We gave Tom the nickname "Tom Bombadil," an affable and mysterious Tolkien character who lives in the forest by himself and enters the story at appropriate moments to aid the Hobbits on their journey. Like Tom Bombadil, our Tom would suddenly appear unannounced in Kota Belud, although instead of helping us, I think we "helped" him, by shocking him with injections of English and 1960s counter-culture.

After an all-day hike, we reached a rudimentary wooded cabin at 11,000 feet (3,353 meters). We lit a campfire in the evening as the temperature dropped to freezing. Fortunately, the interior of the cabin was equipped with a woodstove. We tried to get some sleep for our ascent of the summit the next morning, knowing we had to get up at 4:00 a.m. for an early start to beat the usual midday cloud, rain, and strong winds.

When we reached the top, Low's Peak, around 9:00 a.m., our efforts were rewarded by a 360-degree view of North Borneo. For a moment, I was the highest man in Southeast Asia. I could see the peninsula at Kudat jutting into the Sulu Sea, Kota Belud Valley, and a wide expanse of the South China Sea. Labuan Island bulged into its deep blue waters. Looking in the direction of Sarawak and to the south towards Kalimantan, a sea of green

5.5 Mr. Yeoh on summit below the Donkey's Ears

extended as far as the eye could see. Brilliant white clouds were rapidly forming above the jungle's canopy as tons of water rose into the atmosphere, preparing for the afternoon's downpour.

We wrote our names in the record book and descended to the smooth granite surface to rest in the sun before resuming our exploration. When we got up, we took multiple photos, including some of the famous "Donkey's Ears," a twin-peak formation. From Kota Belud, Mount Kinabalu looks like a solid iron ship floating in the jungle with its bow pointing to the west. Exploring the summit plateau, we could see that the ship was split in half by a deep gorge, dropping some 3,000 feet (914 meters)—surely the chasm which the often-mentioned mythical dragon fell into.

When we grew tired of exploring, we lay down to rest again

with our backs flat on the warm rock and began to daydream, feeling the *aki* all around us—Kadazan-Dusun for "spirits." But our park guide disturbed us too soon. He could feel the building wind and humidity in the air. Our time was up. If we had stayed much longer, the daily deluge would have washed all of us off this plateau. As we lay there, I remember thinking how easy it would be to join the *aki* of the mountain—just stay on the summit until it was too late. I might even meet the abandoned Kadazan-Dusun lady's spirit. Instead, I descended to safety with the others, mission accomplished.

I FOUND LESS physically challenging ways of escaping the confines of Kota Belud. On Friday nights, after a long and tiring week of teaching, Peter and I would smoke a little *ganja* and take our motorcycle over the narrow roads, passing *kampongs* and *padi* fields, *sarong*-clad women and naked children bathing by wells or in streams. We would negotiate narrow paths through herds of cattle bedding down for the night on the warm tarmac, zoom past horses grazing on the plains beside the sea, feel the moist evening breeze on our faces, and witness the rising moon's glow on thatched roofs, harmoniously entering a state of *makan angin*—Malay for "eating the wind" or "doing nothing," implying no obligations, and no need to worry about time and space.

I had experienced such cool breezes on my shirt at the age of 16, when I purchased an old Triumph motorcycle. It was practically disassembled with many parts in a box, so it only cost me 75 Canadian dollars. I rebuilt the motor, reassembled and painted the frame in orange, and decorated the gas tank with red flames. I carefully nurtured that motorcycle through two summers.

Unfortunately, the old Norton that Peter and I purchased had seen better days and broke down frequently. The sight of an *orang putih* with a stalled motorcycle on the roadside, wrenches and screwdrivers in dirty hands, sweating and muttering curses, provided a spectacle for a gathering crowd and no end of comments and laughter. Sometimes audience members offered help. Such happenings increased my ability to speak in Malay...and to laugh at myself.

Our motorcycle also facilitated monthly weekend escapes to KK. I found this necessary because it was almost impossible to talk or mix with single young women in Kota Belud. Had I taken that alternative posting in a Christian Kadazan town, it might have been easier to mix. In fact, a number of foreigners had married Kadazan women, unions usually sanctioned by parents and community elders.

In Kota Belud, the District Officer sometimes held receptions and parties, but these mainly consisted of females sitting on one side of the room and males on the other. Attendees seldom moved, except for filling plates or getting drinks. Recorded Malaysian music followed dull speeches but with no dancing and no alcohol—only orange or lemon squash, a sweet, thick syrup, which we mixed with water.

I loved Chinese New Year—a three-day celebration when I was invited to my Chinese students' homes for fireworks and many-course meals—a continuous feast, moving from house to house, washing down the food with brandy or sweet plum wine. I put on weight that was difficult to lose, but I got to know some of my Chinese students in a more informal way.

I had to try hard to make my beautiful female students off-limits, although they were only four or five years my junior. For a time, I dropped into the family shop of one of my most attractive Chinese students, just to chat. However, I soon recognized that the scowl on her older brother's face was aimed at me. I knew that any indiscreet and excessive attention could start tongues wagging and ruin the girl's reputation, so I phased out these visits. At any rate, her parents sent her away to boarding school to finish her secondary education. This was, I discovered, a common strategy to protect well-developed teenage girls for families who could afford it, so I don't think I caused her departure.

When Peter and I took weekend breaks in KK, we would usually leave right after Friday classes. We'd sleep on other volunteers' couches or mats on their floors. KK was a small city, but large in contrast to Kota Belud, and we enjoyed its exciting features: Tanjong Aru Beach and its restaurants full of modern men and women, the brightly lit night markets on downtown streets, and Chinese nightclubs with sexy female singers from Hong Kong.

In the '60s and '70s, even Muslim women in Malaysia wore tight, shapely skirts and blouses, called *baju kebaya*, with brightly colored batik patterns. It wasn't until the late 1970s, a decade after my time in Kota Belud, that conservative political Islam would infiltrate the country, along with oil money from the Middle East. This outward show of beauty would be snuffed out by means of community pressure and gradually implemented restrictive customs. Fortunately, the non-Muslim population remained free of those impositions.

The weekend trips that Peter and I took to KK acted as our pressure release valve. On Saturday mornings, I'd go to the Chartered Bank to withdraw money, but also to make eyes with one of the most intriguing Chinese women I had ever seen. She smiled at me but remained an unattainable goddess. She could have been married, for all I knew. I think she was just playing with me and really thought of me as an *Ang Mo*, literally, "red haired foreign devil" in Hokkien. I could only dream about her.

Luckily, one weekend, I met Julitah, a Kadazan woman who worked as a maid in a friend's apartment. She was pretty and petite with well-proportioned breasts and flowing curves. She had long black hair, dark eyes, milk-chocolate skin, and one golden tooth. Our eyes met several times on my visit to her boss's house, and we began to chat in Malay. She flirted and my heart raced.

Her employers were going out of town on vacation that day, so I asked Julitah if she wanted me to come back later—"*Balik nanti?*"

"*Balik pukul lapan,*" she smiled, asking me to return at 8:00 p.m.

I came back on my motorcycle in the dark and parked down the hill. I tapped on the door, but there was no answer. I went to the side of the apartment and peered through the louvered bedroom windows, where I saw her sleeping on the bed, exhausted from her day of cooking and cleaning. I called her name and she got up to let me in.

We talked in simple terms about who she was and who I was. She allowed me to touch her. She removed her *sarong*. I undressed. We lay together, joking for some time. She giggled a lot, and I found that sexy. She was an experienced woman, so we took our time. Finally, we climaxed and lay there looking at each other, but we must have made too much noise. We soon heard some students from the nearby dormitory laughing by the window. Had they been spying on us? I waited until they grew tired of their game before I kissed Julitah goodbye. My main concern was to protect her reputation…and her job.

Thus, began my relationship with a woman who expected only tenderness and adventure. I have no photos of her, only the beginnings of a poem—an artifact of my emotions at the time. She was deluded enough to think I looked like a Western movie star, while I saw her as a beautiful and somewhat innocent entrance into the enchanted garden of another culture.

She told me she was born as an animist, became a Christian, and then converted to Islam to marry a Muslim man. Later, he threw her out, simply declaring three times that he was divorcing her, as is the traditional Islamic custom. Her mother cared for her two children back in the village, while Julitah earned money for their upbringing and education.

We had to be very discreet about our times and places of

meeting. Many locals would assume she was a prostitute if seen with me. We spent a night together in a small hotel, ordered meals from the restaurant below, talked, and made love. Sabah didn't have television in those days, and we didn't need such distractions.

Our relationship flourished, then gradually faded due to distance and impracticalities. I knew our educational and cultural gulf could never really be bridged. My vocabulary and confidence in speaking Malay increased dramatically during those periodic weekend liaisons, but not enough to fully grasp the exact details of her past. During our last meeting, she told me her former husband was trying to get her back, so I concluded it was time for me to "exit stage left." The next day, I had the worrying sensation that I was being followed—probably just my paranoia.

Julitah, with her brown skin, golden tooth and earrings, long black hair, and contagious laugh, broke down many of my barriers and inhibitions. Navigating my love affair with her, and exploring the mountain and myths of her people, are my most special memories of bonding with Borneo.

6

Going Native

6.1 A Kadazan farmer surveys his home valley

THE OTHER MOURNERS were telling stories about him as we
squatted around his corpse—a custom that seemed too intimate
to me, with my Canadian Methodist upbringing. Our group fell
silent as the Imam washed Headmaster Anderson's body with the
help of other men. As previously mentioned, Anderson was from
Australia but had converted to Islam since his arrival in Sabah. I

could hear the wails and sobs of his Bajau wife coming from an adjacent room. (In Islam, the preparation of a body for burial must be carried out and witnessed by people of the same gender as the deceased.) The men put their hands under Anderson's hefty milk-white cadaver, flipped it over like a Great White Shark on the deck of a ship, and began to cleanse his backside.

Deputy Headmaster Kumar sat cross-legged beside me. He seemed lost in thought, staring through the open window on the other side of the room. Did he also have difficulty in such intimacy with a corpse? In his Hindu religion, they cremated the dead. Or was he watching for Anderson's spirit to depart through that window? Could it have been something more mundane, like next year's class schedule, which Anderson had asked him to complete? I was supposed to help Kumar draft it, but he'd avoided me for weeks.

Kumar appeared to wake from his daydream as the Imam's last prayer ended. We watched as Anderson's body was wrapped in white linen—all except for his head. The effect of this cover was a relief to me. He had been a heavyset man in his early 60s with thick, black, horn-rimmed glasses that magnified his eyeballs. He wore his thinning gray hair slicked straight back. His pink face always appeared clean shaven in public. He usually wore a white shirt, black shorts and black or gray knee-socks. On Fridays, he exchanged his colonial pith helmet for a white skullcap to attend prayers at the local mosque.

At the end of the cleansing ritual, Anderson's body was placed in a simple wooden box. Two women escorted his Bajau widow from the adjoining room to see him for the last time. She was short and dressed in a black *baju kebaya* and lace headscarf. Her face, once smooth, was now deepened with grief, accentuating her wrinkles. The other women held her up as she tried to flail her arms, crying shrilly in Malay, "*Allah! Apa yang saya akan buat sekarang?*" (Oh, God! What will I do now?) The Imam allowed her one final lamentation, then signaled to take her out of the room.

I stared at Anderson's milk-white face one last time before the men covered it with a white cloth. They placed the lid on the box and we joined in lifting it from below—no handles provided—and carried it downstairs to a small truck waiting in the lane. Muslim custom requires burial before sunset on the same day as death, if possible, and it was getting late. Anderson had died the evening before, so now it was essential to beat the sun.

I had learned of Anderson's death that Saturday morning while in KK with Peter. It was mid-December 1968, and we were enjoying a break after marking year-end exams. We rushed back on our motorcycle as quickly as possible over the 50-mile stretch of tarmac to Kota Belud. We had coasted down the final long hill into Kota Belud Valley and gone directly to Anderson's house—no time to shower and change clothes. Now that the cleansing ceremony was over, we remounted our motorcycle and followed the procession through the town center and out the other side to the Muslim cemetery. When we arrived, two men were still digging Anderson's grave.

The funeral party assembled. A few men plunked the temporary coffin on the ground beside the hole. To me, the whole procedure seemed too quick and lacked any element of ceremony—no reverence, no solemnity. Very few people had a chance to view Anderson's body, and no one present wept for him. Women were not allowed to participate in Muslim burials, so the funeral party consisted of some senior male teachers and students, along with a few district officials. We stood, chatting about Anderson sudden death. The only person I can clearly remember in the group is Kumar. He still seemed to be elsewhere, planning something. I wondered what schemes he was cooking up for our school.

As Anderson's shrouded corpse was removed from the wooden box and lowered into the ground, the group fell silent. I thought of his first wife, who had remained in Australia. I wondered what she knew about his conversion to Islam and his taking a second wife. As a Muslim, he could have four, at least in theory. The first wife is supposed to agree to any additions, but I doubted that this was the case.

Apparently, a telegram had arrived from Australia, giving the go-ahead for the burial. I speculated that she thought this is what Anderson deserved for his behavior, to be buried on an obscure hillside in Borneo, an unmarked grave on top of which other corpses would be placed in a few years, as is the Muslim custom. Did she care at all? What had brought him to this faraway outpost? Whatever quarrel he had had with her, I thought, would remain hidden in his grave.

The sun was setting as the Imam recited his last Quranic verse. I could see that everyone was getting a little edgy. When the Imam signaled it was over, the participants left very quickly, except for the two grave diggers who remained to fill in the hole.

There was something in the air that no one wanted to talk about. Perhaps it was the unspoken feeling that Anderson didn't belong here, that his *hantu* might be destined to haunt Kota Belud forever, contributing to the already rich body of ghost stories that made adults shiver and stole sleep from children: the headless ghost that periodically floated out of the jungle on the road to Tamparuli; the local Chinese man who was jilted by his lover, committed suicide, and appeared at night to some women in town; and the lost souls of over two thousand British and Australian soldiers who were marched to their deaths through the jungle by the Japanese Army during the last months of World War II. Was it Anderson's destiny to join these unfortunate wandering spirits?

In spite of his colonial adherence to school schedules and

specified deadlines—habits beyond the comprehension of Kumar—Anderson had not really been traditional at all. I didn't know him well, but I guessed that he had left Australia out of boredom after obligatory retirement from a career in education. He probably had fallen so much in love with the rhythm of life in Kota Belud that he'd decided to stay. As headmaster of our secondary school, he had lived a new life of relative privilege, honored by the Bajau, Iranun, and Kadazan native leaders, as well as many in the Chinese community.

Only one other relic of British colonial times remained in Kota Belud—Mr. Charrington, an engineer who worked for the Public Works Department. When he wasn't supervising mechanics, plumbers, and electricians, he fraternized with Chinese *towkays*, playing *mah-jongg*. I seldom saw him. In fact, I think he avoided other expats as much as possible. He was definitely a Somerset Maugham kind of character, hanging on long after the last ship of the empire had departed for Liverpool. Such Brits knew they had a good thing going in the former colonies: friendly local people who could be cheaply employed for menial tasks; a car, and maybe a driver; plenty of delicious food and drinking companions; and no dreary, everlasting rain and cold. North Borneo is truly a "land below the wind," as coined in the title of that colonial memoir I had read on the way to Sabah. Maybe Charrington had also read it before he came.

Anderson would have remained just another *orang putih* like Charrington, hanging on in a former colonial outpost, had it not been for his "transformation." To my mind, there was no other way to say it, for Anderson was the most bizarre example in my experience of an expatriate "going native."

I never knew his Bajau wife's name, since he never presented her in public. She was about 10 or 15 years his junior, and rumors floated about town that she had made her living by less than respectable ways after the death of her first husband. I understood this to be typical "blame the victim" gossip in a male-dominated society. Probably she had been destitute.

I concluded that Anderson had believed his long-term position as headmaster would be in jeopardy through an informal arrangement, so he asked the senior local Imam for instruction and converted to Islam in order to marry her, and then moved her into his house. But to secure his position and his stay in Sabah for the rest of his life, he and his new wife made a *haj* to Mecca, a pilgrimage all good Muslims are supposed to take before they die, if they have the means and the health to do so.

By this move, "Haji Anderson," as he came to be known, had risen so much in stature in the eyes of the politically powerful Muslims in the district and state, that his continued status as headmaster was assured. All this had happened before my arrival and, from what I could gather, there had been no advanced warnings about his conversion, marriage, or *haj*. Nor did Anderson ever talk about it or try to justify his decisions to others. Religion was, quite rightly, a private matter to him.

By the time I arrived in Kota Belud, the town was abuzz with jokes and rumors about Anderson's new arrangements. I could only glean a little of what the talk was all about by grilling Hu Hee Bit, the owner of the restaurant where we ate: Could he keep up with a younger woman? Would his heart be able to take it? How long would he last? Apparently, the discussions grew so intense that those who frequented the drinking shops in town began to place bets on the number of days Anderson had left.

Had Anderson's transformation ended with his conversion and marriage, the gossip might not have been so wild; however, shortly after his arrival in Kota Belud, he began to turn a couple of mild habits into apparent addictions. It was most evident at Chinese weddings, to which, as headmaster, he was invariably invited. The frequent calls for *yum sing* or "bottoms up" with the brandy glass had become more and more comfortable, in spite of the fact that these drinks made his normally pink complexion turn beet red, possibly due to a blood pressure problem.

Brandy had also provided a path to a greater passion. Following Charrington, Anderson had taken up *mah-jongg* in the back rooms of Chinese shops, the favorite place for this indulgence. His habit of imbibing brandy while playing the game grew considerably, although both acts are *haram*—forbidden under Islamic law. He couldn't read the *mah-jongg* tiles but was able to recognize many, or at least thought he could. Since he couldn't converse in any of the Chinese languages spoken in town, without his knowing during these games, his companions would often switch from Malay to Chinese in order to place bets on his earthly duration. The stakes were never high. Most of his co-players entered the game for amusement rather than monetary gain.

In spite of his new habits, Anderson managed to maintain both his position and his reputation, at least on the surface. He never arrived late for any appointment or occasion and always kept his part of any bargain. To many of the townspeople, it was quite obvious what had happened to this decent man. Forces beyond his control were responsible for his changes—a *pugai* had been placed on him. In Kota Belud, this form of magic spell explained almost any sudden or unforeseen changes in human behavior or fortune.

The strongest forms of *pugai* were sexual in nature, administered by a woman on an unsuspecting man. One method my teacher friend Winston told me about involved a woman placing a bowl of steaming rice directly under her uncovered vagina immediately before serving it to her unsuspecting male victim. Most people in Kota Belud believed that such a *pugai* had sealed Anderson's fate. In fact, the townspeople repeated and embellished the *pugai* story with great gusto and glee. Since Anderson was not responsible for what had happened to him, his transgressions were forgiven. Besides, he was the supreme educational authority in the district and had considerable influence on the future of all sons and daughters attending school.

When we left the cemetery, I dropped off Peter at a friend's house. I drove towards town, following Kumar in his light brown 1962 Saab. As usual, he was in a hurry. He never landed in one place for long, like a dragonfly in search of prey. He always drove erratically, darting around the cattle, goats, and dogs, which perpetually populated the narrow roads. While seated stiffly in his Saab, chin cocked upwards as if commanding an armored personnel carrier, tooting his horn frequently, as is the habit in India, he remained oblivious to the disapproving scowls of Bajau and Kadazan tribesmen.

By the time I arrived, Kumar had been in Sabah for about five years on a contract with the Department of Education. He held a Master's Degree in Biology from Madras. He always dressed impeccably in a white shirt, black or white shorts, and contrasting knee socks, while sporting perfectly polished black leather shoes. He was in his mid-40s and a man of average height for a native of Southern India. He combed his hair straight back and held it in place with coconut oil, the aroma of which mixed with his strong cologne. He had dark skin and a thin, finely trimmed mustache. The betel nut he chewed had permanently stained his lips and mouth a deep red.

Kumar's sudden accelerations and decelerations on the road matched the spurts of his speech. As sounds emerged from his vocal cords, they were transformed by his rapidly waving tongue so that only the most discerning could make out what he was saying. His words came with such frequency and flurry that the reasoning behind them could not be entirely understood.

Kumar just had one reply for those who tried to penetrate his reality with new information: he would utter, "thatiswhatIsaid." When I finally recognized the meaning of this ejaculation, which came with such speed and frequency, I could only assume that he had said and done almost everything there was to say and do, had seen almost everything this universe has in store for us, and was, therefore, most likely on his hundredth cycle of reincarnation. For instance, when I asked him a simple question about the class schedule: "Mr. Kumar, could I suggest a few changes to the schedule which would make it easier for teachers' timetables next year?"

Kumar's red tongue sputtered forth a torrent of words: "We are having a very difficult one Mr. Neill so many things to consider but I am having thinking of all factors and it is the way I have been doing before in India so not to worry Mr. Neill as the schedule will proceed and be completed with your help and input from many quarters and it will be so excellent I cannot tell you in a few words how excellent since I do not have the time right now but if you are worrying you should not be worrying any longer because I am assuring you all is in hand and we will be ready soon for the new school year that is for sure as I can give you my word on that Mr. Neill."

"So, I can make a few suggestions?"

"ThatiswhatIsaid."

I had come to the conclusion that Kumar must have been pleased when Anderson had married a local woman, for it appeared he had followed Kumar's own lead in an interracial match. As far as I knew, Kumar had arrived in Sabah as a bachelor. He had married a Chinese woman during his first posting and had brought her to Kota Belud. They were very private. No one I knew had ever been invited to their house. His wife didn't mix with the shopkeepers' wives, so she became the subject of much gossip. The most widely held rumor was that she was an older, unmarried daughter and that Kumar had purchased her for a low bride price. Others whispered a *pugai* had caused this marriage, too.

I reached the town center and pulled up on my motorcycle in front of Hu Hee Bit's restaurant just as I saw Kumar speeding off in his Saab on the road to our school. I wanted to find out for myself about the circumstances that had led to Anderson's death the evening before. In the back rooms of some shops, I could hear the clinking of *mah-jongg* chips, mixed with newly invigorated gossip.

I tried to piece together the story from Hu. His predominant conclusion was that Anderson's heart had given out. He had fallen on the floor and convulsed after winning for the first time in months. Hu told me there were rumors floating about town that Anderson had been poisoned by his Bajau wife after he told her he had decided to return to his wife in Australia. But this made no sense to me. Anderson seemed so happy in Sabah and, besides, he'd provided his new wife with a kind of respectability, an income, and security. Surely, he would have taken care of her, regardless.

Perhaps it was the sheer excitement of winning, perhaps the brandy, or both. Ironically, he had been fasting during the day—like a good Muslim should do during the holy month of *Ramadan*. Too hard on his system? He didn't die in bed as many had predicted. But it was vehemently argued by some that his new wife was still the real cause. His heart couldn't take it! What could you expect? A man of his age....

As the evening progressed and the brandy and beer flowed, gossip turned to banter and banter to arguments over who had bet what and who had won. To the *mah-jongg* players, there was no disrespect in this, and no conclusion was ever reached. Anderson loved betting, and he would surely have wagered on his own life had they only let him in on their gossip. Kota Belud had no cinema, so these stories provided the greatest source of entertainment. Any definite conclusion would be a dead-end, with little chance for greater embellishment, and where was the fun in that?

After learning all I could for one evening, I returned home to reflect on the day's events. I sat on my veranda above the starlit valley, cogitating upon the death of Anderson. He had been a fair and straightforward man, my first boss since graduating from university. Now, with Kumar in charge, we had to prepare for a period of confusion. I hoped that Anderson would be replaced by someone like him, with the skills and knowledge needed to run things smoothly in this multi-racial, complex, and politically important place.

I wondered what Kumar was up to. There was only a week of school left before his planned departure for a vacation in India. I mused that he was probably experiencing some liberation now that Anderson was gone—plenty of time to complete the schedule before January, when classes would resume. To Kumar, Anderson had been like a colonial master, demanding things long before they were really needed. Kumar usually responded at the last minute to Anderson's demands, and his schedules and other inputs were inevitably so "mumble-jumble" that someone had to fix them. There was nothing I could do about it until January, so I decided I should just go with the flow and enjoy my planned vacation.

In my bedroom, as I lay in the moist air under the mosquito net and pulsating ceiling fan, Anderson's rotting fish-like corpse, now under a few feet of cold earth, clouded my thoughts. Was it really a transformation, or had he just been an old fool who had lost his rudder? Did he ever have any regrets? Is this what happens when you stay too long in such far-flung outposts? Do you lose yourself bit by bit and end up going native in a crazy way? Or did he truly find himself? Who was I to judge?

Finally, I drifted into a deep sleep while the cattle grazed on the grass outside, occasionally knocking their horns on the underside of our raised bungalow.

MY DREAMS that night propelled me into a dreamlike vacation. It became real when I packed a light duffle bag, drove to KK, and flew to Labuan Island to take a freighter called "The Rajah Brooke" over the South China Sea to Singapore. I stayed for three Singapore dollars (1.80 USD) a night at the Veena-Meena Hotel and talked at length to the Tamil proprietor's attractive daughter. I ate cheap South Indian *thali*, a variety of vegetarian curries served on banana leaves with mounds of rice and unlimited *chapati* and *naan*, tasty flatbreads. I wandered through the shops and streets, looking at things I had no need for, nor money to buy.

One evening, I walked under a bamboo scaffold-type structure and entered an open area to witness a Chinese opera. People sat on plastic chairs on the street or on the balconies of shophouses, watching the spectacle. I joined them, listening to shrill Cantonese song and speech backed by Chinese lute and punctuated by clashing cymbals. The rich aroma of *joss* sticks filled the air. I became mesmerized by the bright red, gold, and black costumes of ancient China. The audience laughed and called out to the players. I felt so foreign.

The next day, I took a train north into West Malaysia, traveling through rubber plantations and small towns to the nation's capital, Kuala Lumpur, known as KL. (*Kuala* means "confluence" and *lumpur* means "mud" in Malay. No one swam in the murky waters that joined there.) I checked into a cheap hotel in the Chinese Quarter and went out to wander. I studied the window of a Buddhist vegetarian shop displaying a half-dozen soya-bean chickens hanging on hooks. I walked through brightly lit street displays of food, clothes, cosmetics, hardware, and tapes of pirated music. When I sat down to eat at a food stall, the guy beside me smiled and greeted me warmly. We talked a while, and he invited me to his home to meet his family. I accepted, and the next day I shared in a great Chinese Christmas feast. I believe his only motivation was that he felt no apparent Christian should be alone on that day.

Later that week, I traveled to Port Dickson to swim in the Straits of Malacca, where I bumped into James, a CUSO volunteer from my group who had been posted to Sarawak. We traveled by bus together to the City of Malacca. Its orange-tiled roofs and shops of ancient Chinese furniture and European artifacts were remnants of the time when Portuguese traders made this port one of their principal stops between Europe and China. James was a good traveling companion, but I thought he was smoking a little too much *ganja*—frequently drifting into an inner world. We returned to Singapore to catch separate ships. James returned to Kuching, while I sailed back to Labuan.

By that time, I had almost forgotten my little town near the coast of Sabah, Anderson's funeral, and the unfinished class schedule. I had become totally absorbed in the sights, sounds, smells, and tastes of a much larger and more exotic world.

I remained in such an innocent state until early January, when I returned to Kota Belud. Kumar also came back, but not only from India. He had converted to Islam, traveled to Mecca, and now had a new name, "Haji Abdul bin Abdullah," although we continued to just call him "Mr. Kumar."

Upon the revelation of this latest transformation, I resolved to be on guard against any bowls of rice from questionable sources during the rest of my sojourn in Sabah.

7

Dog Days

7.1 Kota Belud during an unusual dry season, January to May, 1969

OUR CREATION of the NBFS proved to be an antidote for Peter, Caitie, and me—protection from a darkness that had begun to advance over the land in early 1969. When the school year began, we entered a period of chaos. Secondary school enrollment had nearly doubled, but there had been little planning and preparation for this influx of students. Many of the West Malaysian teachers had finished their service in Sabah and had gladly headed home. The Department of Education promised reinforcements, but after many weeks only one appeared, a Tamil-Malaysian fellow by the name of Edward. That left Peter, Caitie, Kumar, Edward, and me to cope with almost two hundred students—up to forty per class. Kumar assigned us to work double shifts, teaching from 7:30 a.m. through the afternoons until 5:00 p.m., with just a short lunch break—a grinding schedule, even heavier than North American high schools.

I found the extra workload tiring but fulfilling. I enjoyed the extended contact with my students' budding minds. But we all missed Anderson. He had demonstrated a strict but steady hand in school affairs. The Department of Education had appointed Kumar as acting headmaster, and we had his muddle-headed management to contend with, until—we hoped—a new headmaster would arrive.

Kumar taught science, but I heard from some students that they couldn't understand him. I overheard him teaching and realized their problem. He spoke rapidly in his heavily accented English, using a lot of university-level jargon. "We are having an osmotic process which is inhibited only to the degree of temperature variation within the system. But we already covered that one yesterday, isn't it?" Looking in at the students through the louvered windows, I saw a sea of blank faces.

By mid-January, the West Coast of Sabah had entered a prolonged dry spell, the only one I can remember during my stay. The wind would pick up by midday, blowing dust from the barren plain that surrounded our school. I could feel it entering my mouth whenever I spoke. The heat put everyone on edge. Some of the Bajau boys began to test our authority by leaving school whenever they wanted to, just showing up to collect their scholarship money. I got angry with a particularly lazy student and they all saw "Mr. Nail's" fierce side. I think that helped me keep things under control.

Ramadan was over, the fasting month when Muslims are not supposed to eat or drink from sunup to sundown—not even swallow their own saliva. But due to the dust, some Muslim boys

7.2 Government Secondary School, Kota Belud, in the dry season

continually got up to go outside and spit on the ground during classes. Although I found this practice disgusting, I decided to say nothing, lest I offend.

One of the greatest impediments to progress in getting through the syllabus was the numerous holidays: *Hari Rayat Puasa* (the end of *Ramadan*), Prophet Mohammed's birthday, the Agong's birthday, Kadazan Harvest Festival, Chinese New Year, and on and on. The school closed for all of these holidays to respect each culture. In addition, Kumar used his authority to call discretionary holidays at any time. The so-called "Sports Day" took the kids out of class for three days of competition held in the scorching sun.

I had a misunderstanding with some students over Sports Day. I had been appointed housemaster of the student group called *Rumah Badak* (House of the Rhinoceros). We carefully designed all the sports teams to be of mixed ethnicity. In the spirit of healthy competition, I bravely took my minimal artistic skills to the blackboard. I prepared a colored drawing of a *badak* (rhino)

standing on a *singa* (lion) and a *harimau* (tiger), while slaying a
naga (dragon). As soon as the students saw it, a few became very
angry with me. One boy posted a written notice, claiming that
I was trying to divide students and bring about fights. I had to
apologize and erase what I had thought to be just a humorous
cartoon. I quickly learned that in this multi-ethnic environment,
it was nearly a declaration of open warfare to speak against another team, even in jest.

During this time, my friend Winston sent a Bajau girl home
because she hadn't completed her homework. Her father soon
showed up at the school with a *parang*, threatening to kill Winston, who wisely fled. It was as if Winston had dishonored the
whole Bajau people by his action. Kumar didn't defend him at all.
He wavered this way and that, agreeing with whomever he talked
to last, merely repeating his favorite phrase, "thatiswhatIsaid."

Although we foreign teachers didn't feel particularly threatened, this incident only heightened non-local Malaysian teachers'
desire "to get out of Dodge" as fast as possible. Word spread, further inhibiting the posting of more teachers to Kota Belud. And
so, our teacher-student ratio remained a problem.

In some ways, our town with its Bajau horsemen was like the
Old West of America, substituting the *parang* for the six-gun.
Some people took, or threatened to take, the law into their own
hands by accusing their enemies of defamation. The "sheriff"
could be called, but he had only so much power. Most of the
fights just involved posturing and flexing of muscles, but such
threats kept everyone on edge.

One Saturday at exactly 6:00 a.m., I woke to tremendous
blasts of shotguns, and I wondered if a revolution had begun.
I soon discovered it was what I later called "dog day." On one
day every year, the local police devoted about eight hours to
shooting stray dogs. For most Muslims, dogs and pigs are at the
same low level of existence—unclean animals. On "dog day," the

Chinese quickly pulled any pet dogs inside their gates and tied, chained, or caged them. But strays had no such cover. The firing continued until mid-afternoon, or whenever the executioners considered the excess population sufficiently culled. Meanwhile, canine corpses piled up on roadsides around town until sanitation workers, with handkerchiefs tied around their noses, arrived to hoist the fly-ridden carcasses onto a lorry (a truck, in North American parlance).

Afterwards, I noticed that fewer dogs gathered to procreate under the streetlight below our house. We experienced some relief from the nocturnal barking, growling, and yelping of males fighting over bitches. The successful ones worked themselves into a frenzy and got stuck. But in a few days, the surviving dogs returned. I came to understand that "dog day" was a game of survival of the fittest and the most fecund. The smarter creatures would head for the jungle with the first blasts, returning when the gunfire ceased and it was once again safe to continue the search for sustenance in human garbage by day, and to breed by night.

In May of 1969, Kota Belud's "dog day" morphed into Malaysia's political "dog days," the heated exchanges and bloody riots during the first phase of the national election. Despite the presence of Chinese and Indian settlers in the Malayan Peninsula, dating back hundreds of years, as modernization and economic development continued in the twentieth century, tension grew between the *bumiputera*—the majority Malays and other indigenous people—and the Chinese and Indian populations. Leading up to the May 10th elections in West Malaysia, some opposition parties, dominated by Chinese (mostly Buddhists or Christians) and Indians (mainly Hindu), had staged a strong campaign against the Malay-dominated ruling Alliance Party (mainly Muslim), whose key platform was one of affirmative action for the *bumiputera*.

The Chinese, who had the greatest share of the economy, and

the Indians, at the bottom of the economic and social ladder, resented this official favoritism. The governing Alliance won less than half of the popular vote, although it still held a majority of seats in Parliament; whereas, the opposition parties, dominated by Chinese and Indians, made significant gains and celebrated their achievements in "victory" marches.[1]

Many rumors swirled around what followed. As I later discovered after reading some banned newsmagazine reports handed around by foreign volunteers, the period became a full and fearful demonstration of the English-Malay phrase, "run *amok*." On May 13, in Kuala Lumpur, taunts and jeers escalated into fistfights and destruction, as Malays burned cars and property in Chinese neighborhoods. Over the next few days, Malay mobs killed hundreds of Chinese and Indians with *parangs*, clubs, and stones.

The Malays mounted frenzied responses against this challenge to their favored position in the post-colonial power structure. Some Chinese and Indian factions counter-attacked, killing and injuring many Malays. Fortunately, Malaysia's strict firearm control laws prevented the death toll from rising even higher. The government declared a national emergency and suspended parliament. Eventually, Tunku Abdul Rahman, Malaysia's first Prime Minister, was forced to resign. A caretaker government remained in charge until 1971.

During the upheaval, the state governments of Sabah and Sarawak postponed voting. In Sabah, we held our breath, praying that the riots would not boil over into our towns. The Chief Minister all but outlawed opposition parties. The lid held tight on a boiling pot. We breathed a collective sigh of relief. I heard, once more, the songs of the colorful birds of Borneo calling out for peace.

Before "dog day" in Kota Belud and the news and rumors of what happened in KL, I think I had grown into an innocent and heightened euphoric state, at one with all the sights, sounds, smells, and tactile sensations of my new social and physical environment—a kind of heaven. But I had now experienced a different version of Malaysia—a taste of hell.

During this period of my stay in Malaysia, I had the opportunity to venture out of my self-protective cavern. I experienced life as it is. The doors of perception were indeed cleansed for me. I had awakened to an acceptance of the new realities and features of this vibrant, rainbow-colored land, as well as the darker, Mordor-like shadows that could roll over it at any time. My senses opened, recording it all, and that would become my new preoccupation.

8

Borneo through
a New Lens

8.1 Flora at the foot of Mount Kinabalu

IN SABAH, MY ACCENTUATED perception led me into a new vocation—making movies. I liked some parts of teaching, especially
how my students were keen on learning and appreciative of my
so-called "sacrifice" in giving two years of my life to their education. I judged myself to be a pretty good teacher, but I found
the task of getting through the information-loaded, exam-driven

syllabus tedious. The goals involved memorizing facts instead
of solving problems or getting students to explore their immediate environment.

Through a variety of summer jobs—in my dad's factory, in
an iron ore mine, and as an orderly in a mental hospital—I'd
learned that occupations with repetition were not for me. The
daily rhythm of teaching was too predictable. Little did I know
that hanging out with my high-energy, talented colleague, Peter,
would lead me to a lifetime career.

At the time, Peter was making a film for the Peace Corps on
the life of American volunteers in Sabah. He had purchased an
old 16mm Bolex movie camera from a film hobbyist by the name
of Chu-Chu, a tailor who had a shop in KK. I could take decent
photos and I had an interest in filmmaking, but next to no experience. I made a deal with Peter to borrow his camera and possibly
to buy it from him later if CUSO took me up on my offer to make
a recruitment film designed to attract more Canadian volunteers
to Malaysia and other countries.

I wrote to the director of the Information Department at
CUSO Ottawa, exaggerating my thin experience in filmmaking.
(Actually, the only film I had ever made was a Super 8mm piece on
my little brother playing, set to Dylan Thomas reading his poem
Fern Hill.) I sent a budget for the expensive 16mm film stock
and processing, postage, and my travel. After a few exchanges
by mail, I received an approval letter to start filming and CUSO
immediately transferred start-up funds for the project to my bank
account in KK. It surprised me how easy it was to make this deal.
They must have been desperate for recruitment materials.

Peter owned a few books on cinematography and filmmaking,
which I devoured before I started filming. He also gave me a few
tips, but I sensed that filmmaking, for him, was a means of subjec-
tive self-expression. However, to me, the old Bolex camera, with
its three turret lenses, was an instrument for uncovering objective

reality. I felt like it belonged in my hands. I borrowed 350 USD from my father to purchase it from Peter, optimistically promising to gradually pay Dad back as soon as my filmmaking career took off, post-Sabah. The Bolex didn't have sound-recording capacity, so I made do with voice-over narration mixed with music in post-production. I produced the title by double exposing the scene of a jet arriving at KK airport on lettering that I'd chalked on a blackboard at school. I created the end credits by superimposing them on a *kerbau* wallowing in the mud. This low-budget production gave me a high-energy channel for exploring and recording Borneo.

I received permission from Acting Headmaster Kumar to take a little time off to travel to other parts of Sabah for my project. My meager salary would not have allowed such travel without this assignment. I hadn't seen much of other Canadian volunteers since arriving in Sabah. In my opinion, too many of them had been posted to KK. I thought they socialized with one another too much, to the detriment of their relationships with Malaysians. Now, I had the opportunity to visit some of them at their posts, and I would gain new friends.

In July 1969, I flew to the East Coast of Sabah to visit Ron and Mary Hunt, a couple in Sandakan. I filmed Ron teaching auto mechanics and Mary in her secretarial skills class. These subjects, I thought at the time, were more appropriate than those I was teaching in Kota Belud. In retrospect, these early opinions underestimated the upward mobility a general education can bring.

Next, I visited another couple, Andy and Nelly Woodsworth, capturing them on film in their school and in Tawau, a small city near the border of Kalimantan, Indonesia. An added advantage to these filming trips was that, at the same time, I could carry out further mapping and fantasy studies for the NBFS. Tawau is near the site of an extinct volcano, Mount Gemok, which Peter and I surmised must surely be the remains of Tolkien's Mount Doom where, during the Second Age, Sauron lived and forged "The One Ring." Before I left Tawau, I took a taxi to the site of Mount Gemok. Not much was left of it, which made sense, because in Tolkien's story Mount Doom had violently erupted with the final destruction of "The One Ring."

From Tawau, I hired an old but reliable Mercedes taxi, the mainstay vehicle for the 66 miles (106 km) of gravel road to Semporna, a place name that means "beauty to behold." We glided over the bumps at high speed with ease, as if we were flying. In Semporna, I visited and filmed another CUSO teacher, Nana Sakamoto, a Canadian of Japanese descent. I thought Semporna was an isolated and difficult place for a single woman to navigate. It's located on the tip of a peninsula which juts out into the Sulu Sea. Piracy was then, and remains today, a security threat in these waters.

I told Nana how I admired her stamina. We shared our experiences in Bajau communities. Nana lived in the school compound outside of the town center. Her main social contacts were her school community, which consisted of other teachers and their families, and students boarding in the dormitory. But she did get out on excursions to see the land and its people. She thought of Semporna as an incredible adventure in a tropical paradise. She told me that, on arrival, when she was first introduced to the school, the headmaster said she was a Japanese Canadian, but that she looked like a Bajau. However, in my brief observations, in dress, speech, and body language, she was North American and therefore someone to be gawked at, especially by men.

Bajaus make up the majority of the population in Semporna. Many of them live in water villages, groups of houses built on piles over the sea. Thousands of *Bajau Laut* "Sea Gypsies" are attracted to this town. A nomadic people, they live on small boats, fishing and extracting a livelihood from the surrounding coral reefs. Many *Bajau Laut* sail between Sabah and the Philippines to visit family, smuggle, and trade goods in either direction. Some never set foot on dry land until their death and burial in the earth, in accordance with Islamic custom.

I filmed Nana in Semporna on July 20, 1969, the day American astronauts landed on the moon. In my edited film, for contrast, I included a sequence of Nana at her isolated school, set to the soundtrack of Neil Armstrong saying those famous words, "One small step for Man, one giant leap for Mankind." I mentioned in the film's narration how the claim of this landing had been a joke to most Sabahans who heard about it. They were suspicious of reported news, especially outlandish claims on scientific progress—definitely considered, in today's parlance, "fake news."

When I returned to Kota Belud at the end of July, Hu Hee Bit laughed off the moon landing story as a complete fantasy and pure propaganda. *"Mana boleh sampai bulan?"*—how can anyone reach the moon? Many aspects of Chinese culture are centered on traditions about the moon. They celebrate the Harvest Moon Festival in mid-autumn, the eighth month of their lunar calendar, when they eat and give others moon-cakes. There's a legend of a Chinese goddess, Chang-O, who chose to live on the moon. In fact, the command center of Apollo 11 in Houston told the astronauts to look out for her:[1]

> **Houston:** Among the large headlines concerning Apollo this morning, there's one asking that you watch for a lovely girl with a big rabbit. An ancient legend says a beautiful Chinese girl called "Chang-O" has been living there for 4,000 years. It seems she was banished to the Moon because she stole the pill of immortality from her husband. You might also look for her companion, a large Chinese rabbit, who is easy to spot since he is always standing on his hind feet in the shade of a cinnamon tree. The name of the rabbit is not reported.
>
> **Astronaut Buzz Aldrin:** OK. We'll keep a close eye out for the bunny girl.

Had Hu heard about this clowning, it would have been even more evidence for him that the moon landing was all a fantastic movie script, acted out at the expense of his culture.

I had to put off further filming until November and December, when we had seven weeks of school vacation. During that period, I traveled to Sarawak to film an agronomist, medical volunteers, and teachers. When I arrived in Kuching, the state capital, I found a sleepy old town with white buildings, some overgrown with moss. As I walked through large parks with lush lawns and stately trees, thousands of swallows filled the evening air. Unlike KK, with its mainly modern, utilitarian buildings, Kuching struck me to be an old city with a long and storied history, like that of Sarawak itself.

I had read about the history of this place before leaving Canada, including the rise and fall of the Brooke family. For a century, beginning in 1842, they ruled Sarawak as "White Rajahs." The Sultan of Brunei first appointed James Brooke, an Englishman born in British India, as the Governor of Sarawak for his help in crushing a rebellion. Later, when pirates attacked Brunei in large numbers, Brooke and his forces fought them off effectively. The Sultan made him the Rajah of Sarawak, a royal title that remained in the Brooke family until the Japanese invaded in 1942.[2] After the defeat of Japan in 1945, Sarawak became a British colony. Then, in 1963, it joined with Sabah, Singapore, and Malaya, to form Malaysia. (Singapore opted out in 1965.)

At the time of my visit in 1969, a low-level communist insurgency continued in parts of the state. The insurgents, predominantly ethnic Chinese, first opposed British rule and later objected to Sarawak joining Malaysia. Various protected areas called "New Villages"—rural settlements created to control the population from communist influence—made parts of Sarawak feel like a very different land than Sabah. To me, it appeared to be more secretive and more Chinese. The region around the Rajang River provided the most mystery. Rajah Charles Brooke had granted land to many Fuzhou Chinese after the 1900-01 Boxer Rebellion in China. Some Sarawak Chinese in the area still farmed for a living, like peasants in China.[3]

I interviewed and filmed Chris and Gina Smart, a couple posted to Sibu Rural Government Secondary School. They told me that living in their part of Sarawak was more like living in rural China than in Malaysia. The local social scene and culture remained quite closed to foreigners, although as a married couple, they had made some inroads.

I also stopped to see James, the guy I had briefly traveled with in West Malaysia the year before. He was posted to a Chinese Middle School. I found him withdrawn, listening to music, and still smoking too much *ganja*. For him, being somewhat of an introvert, such a posting may have been exactly what he didn't need. A few years later, I learned that he committed suicide after returning to Canada. It seemed like such a crapshoot to me. Would this fellow have suffered such culture shock if he had been posted to a more open part of Malaysia? My memories of him, mostly sitting with his earphones in his room, make me grateful for my posting in the ethnically diverse and more socially mobile "cowboy town" of Kota Belud.

Coming to the end of my filming itinerary, and before taking a pure vacation in Indonesia, I boarded a commercial speedboat destined for Kapit, a town in the Sarawak interior. I rolled my camera more than my film budget could afford, as the boat plied its usual route up the Rajang River. Along the way, I captured a wide variety of images: villagers in watercraft of every variety; pepper vines, fruit trees, and rubber plantations; small farms and increasingly smaller villages; dense jungle and extracted logs floating downstream for export. Towards evening, I caught on film thousands of "flying foxes"—huge fruit bats with wing spans of over five feet (1.5 meters)—as they filled the sky against a crimson sunset.

At Kapit, I hired a boat and a guide to take me to an Iban longhouse. Ibans are a famous people with a rich and much-studied culture. I wanted to find a way to work them into my film. At the time, most Ibans continued to live in traditional communal longhouses, which they built along the rivers on wooden piles for protection against floods, snakes, and beasts of the jungle such as wild boar. While the people lived above, they dropped their kitchen and human waste to their pigs below.

The longhouse I visited measured about 200 feet in length and 50 feet in width (61 by 15 meters). The Ibans constructed it with bamboo floors and walls made of thin *attap*, so privacy for the many families who lived side-by-side was limited—not great for light sleepers or lovers. The sleeping and resting rooms took up one side, while the open space on the other side of the platform served for cooking, eating, social exchange, formal meetings, dances, and ceremonies.

At the time of my visit, some longhouses had turned commercial, catering to increasingly frequent visitors seeking a glimpse of a mysterious culture. In this particular longhouse, a number of human skulls hung in nets along the communal side of the platform. I was informed that Ibans had been encouraged by the Allies, during the war with Japan, to return to their ancient headhunting custom. They targeted Japanese soldiers with poisonous darts shot from blowpipes and severed their heads for trophies. I filmed a sequence on these nets full of skulls, which "decked the halls" while almond-eyed children played amongst them.

Making this first film was, in and of itself, an education for me. To avoid offense, I had to learn to negotiate with people and to communicate my purpose well. Capturing Borneo on celluloid brought new meaning to my life. The view through my lens made me more aware of every element—lighting, color, faces, landscapes, movement, and my relation to all of this.

The following year, when I had the time and facilities to edit my film, I featured this Rajang River journey, ending with the skulls. I set the sequence to *Sometimes in Winter* by the popular music group Blood Sweat and Tears. The exotic images and contrasting words in the music, I mused, might help to encourage more adventurous people to join CUSO, while frightening away others who might not have the mettle to *tahan*, a useful Malay word for "endure" or "stand up to challenges."

For the final lines of narration in my film, I drew on my own experience: "You can do what you want to do. Be what you want to be. You've got two years of summer to do it in."

Indeed, I was following my own advice.

9.1   Batik painting by Bambongodoro Wokidjo (1969)

9

Unpacking the
Batik Painting

WHEN I RETURNED from Indonesia in January of 1970, my house in Kota Belud smelled musty. Mold grows quickly in the tropics when rooms are left closed and unaired. I had been away for almost two months of school vacation, shooting my film and traveling in Indonesia.

Peter had finished his two years in Kota Belud and no other volunteers had been assigned to our school, so I had the house to myself. He'd moved to KK to work on a special education project: a year's extension with the Peace Corps, which ensured another year's reprieve from the war in Vietnam. At least I would get to see him when I visited the capital.

Caitie had also finished her teaching stint, but she'd left Sabah to teach English in Japan, so I could no longer go down the road to see her, have some tea, listen to music, and chat. Peter and Caitie had become my closest friends, true soulmates who shared similar values and perspectives. We laughed at the same things. I already missed that.

I also missed Rebecca, my traveling companion in Indonesia. Before flying to Singapore from Kuching, I had dropped in to see her at her school and invited her to join me in Central Java after her classes ended. I had been somewhat surprised by her spontaneous acceptance. I played my new Bob Dylan LPs on my record player—*Girl from the North Country* and *Lay Lady Lay*. The songs brought back memories of Rebecca.

Listening to the music, I unpacked and sorted my filming equipment and unedited film. I carefully stored everything in the trunk I had brought from Canada, in which I had installed a small light to keep things dry and protected from mold. I took out the only cultural memorabilia I had collected along the way, a batik cloth painting purchased in Yogyakarta, Indonesia. I unfolded it and tacked it to the living room wall. I inspected this orange-black creation—more shocking than I'd remembered—with the artist's name and date inscribed in the bottom right-hand corner: "Bambongodoro Wokidjo 1969."

The whirling ceiling fan caused the batik to shudder and come to life. Its intricate elements rippled, stirring up my experiences during the past month. The four-legged beast at its center lurched downward. Another beast's head, emerging from the upper left, had feline whiskers and scary eyes, but both had ears like delicate butterflies. Strange fish-like creatures with ornamental tails flew in the dark sky. Detached eyes erupted into wing-like patterns. Streams of a bloody lava oozed downwards. The whole scene flowed counter-clockwise, chaos emerging into a kind of symmetry, with pockets of stars pulling me inwards towards the black space of unpacked memories.

A FEW WEEKS earlier, I had been lying on a straw mat on the deck of a freighter, gazing at the stars. I could see the Southern Cross near the horizon. European explorers of long ago, the first to venture into the southern hemisphere, discovered this constellation as guidance in navigating these waters, where they could no longer sight the North Star and the Big Dipper. For me, as for them, it was a beacon in the night sky, inviting me southwards into the unknown.

A few other Western travelers slept near me. The all-Indonesian crew had fed us well and had seen to our bedding needs. I only needed a sheet over me, with a light blanket on standby. I grew sleepy, rocked by the waves of the South China Sea meeting the Java Sea. A warm breeze blew off Sumatra towards Borneo, enveloping me.

In the morning, the sweet smell of clove-scented cigarettes woke me, almost certainly *Dji-sam-soe 234*, the most popular brand in Indonesia at the time. I got up to view our progress from the bow. We'd left Singapore the previous morning and were now well south of the equator, bound for Tanjung Priok, the port serving Jakarta, Indonesia. Passage on this small freighter, which only moved at 10 knots (11.5 mph), cost me around 40 USD, a price that suited my budget. I had about 45,000 Indonesian Rupiah on me, the equivalent of 150 USD. I also had a few more dollars in reserve for my flight home to Sabah; otherwise, all I possessed was my passport, a duffle bag with a few clothes, and my old still camera. In Singapore, I had left my film footage for processing at Kodak and stored my filming equipment with some friends I had met there.

As we sailed farther south, I got to know the freighter's crew. They all appeared to be native Indonesian except for one who looked more Chinese to me. In any case, there was no sense of ethnic division in their interactions. The languages of Indonesia and Malaysia are similar, derived from Malay, the same root language. But some words have different meanings, providing puzzlement and humor in our exchanges. The steward invited me to sleep in the crew's cabin on our second night at sea. I couldn't refuse his hospitality, in spite of the slight smell of diesel permeating the rooms inside the ship.

My ability to communicate with the crew benefited all the travelers. I chatted with the cook, and he made extra efforts for our communal meals. I became the go-to-guy for requests and information on the progress of our voyage. I felt that I belonged.

Before we reached the port, I took a group photo of the crew and we exchanged addresses. They asked me where I would be staying in Jakarta and elsewhere in Indonesia. They became concerned with my answer, "*Saya tidak tahu*," I don't know. For them, only vagrants or homeless people wouldn't know where they were going to sleep. To reassure them, I told them I had the address of a youth hostel in Jakarta, which a traveler in Singapore had recommended. But I had no idea if there would be any room for me there.

The ship docked in Tanjung Priok and we said our goodbyes. I walked towards a group of *bemo* drivers, all competing for my attention. *Bemo* are three-wheel scooter taxis for longer distances. I took the first one and showed my driver the hostel address. We were off with much smoke and fury, an unpleasant contrast to the pure sea air I had just left.

Jakarta was a city of chaos. Driving an ordinary car through this confusion would have been a very specialized job. My *bemo* hit a wall of *bechak*, trishaws in which passengers sit in front as if it were their duty to act as buttresses to oncoming traffic. *Delman* (horse-drawn carts)—some made of old car bodies, axles, and wheels—obstructed progress but added some humor to the scene. My visit occurred before Indonesia's petroleum boom, and these vehicles appeared to be a statement on the need for self-reliance.

When I arrived at the youth hostel, I met a student, Jamil, a handsome guy in his early twenties. He introduced me to Jamsudin, the more senior of the two. I couldn't really figure out who owned the facility or how it ran. They didn't have a register; in fact, they didn't assign a specific room to me. I don't recall meeting any other guests, but when I asked them where I could sleep, I was taken to a poorly screened veranda at the back, where they

9.2 Indonesian freighter crew, my new friends

9.3 With Jamsudin and Jamil in Jakarta

showed me an old wooden door resting on two sawhorses. I was careful not to show any disappointment; after all, how could a poor traveler look such "gift horses" in the mouth? They didn't provide a mattress, not even a pad, nor a mosquito net. At least I would be dry in case of rain.

In the evening, we went out together to a night market for some fish curry and rice. The market was filthy, with garbage strewn all around. I knew I could easily get diarrhea from this hospitality but felt compelled to accompany my friendly hosts.

I probed a bit into what it was they did, what they were studying, and where they came from in Indonesia. They told me they were both from Jakarta itself, but they remained vague about their activities. They briefly mentioned the 1965–66 right-wing coup and revolution the country had gone through, but I couldn't figure out their opinion of, or role in, that upheaval. My lack of vocabulary and our language differences were barriers to better understanding.

After eating, we wandered through the streets. My hosts took me to a one-story house surrounded by a wall. The place radiated with good-looking young Indonesian women. At first, I thought they were sisters or cousins. We joked and laughed and an older "aunty" served us some beer. We sat on plastic chairs in the outside dirt compound, and Jamil passed around a joint of *ganja*. I got a little high.

In spite of my state, or perhaps due to my increased acuity, I soon realized it was a brothel and I was being paired with one of the "sisters." My sexual frustration matched her beauty. Besides, I felt I couldn't refuse my new friends' hospitality. Jamil and Jamsudin also went off to separate rooms with a couple of girls. It seemed like they were having a frequent after-dinner treat.

Making love with this girl was mechanical and unfulfilling. In a couple of minutes, I emerged from the room, immediately regretting the experience. The brothel didn't have any condoms, and I wasn't prepared. I knew I could get gonorrhea or some other sexually transmitted disease from this encounter. I can't remember who paid for this experience—probably my new friends. My own payment was yet to come.

When we returned to the hostel, I told Jamsudin and Jamil that I was tired and would go to sleep. Jamil casually said, "You're safe with us." In unison, they suddenly brandished their pistols and grinned. Alarm bells rang! What had I gotten into with these guys? I could have kicked myself for being so naïve. Most ordinary law-abiding people didn't own handguns in Malaysia or Canada. I doubted if they were allowed in Indonesia. Since it was too late to find other accommodation, and probably too dangerous to go out alone in the dark, I tried to keep my cool and went to my "room and board."

That night, different scenarios darted around in my head as I drifted in a state of semi-consciousness with the sounds of Jakarta traffic, the scuffles of distant dogs, and the drone of mosquitoes penetrating the warm, polluted air. Towards dawn, roosters warned me more than thrice—signs of my impending doom?

At the time, open wounds remained on the land and psyche of Indonesia. Only three years had passed since a band of right-wing generals had overthrown President Sukarno's nationalist government. With the help of the CIA and State Department, the American military had educated and trained these rebels, led by General Suharto who had taken over as President.

Clearly, Sukarno had been too nationalistic, too leftist, and too friendly with Communist China for American tastes in an era when the so-called "domino theory" was still in vogue. Americans believed that if Vietnam was lost to communism, the rest of Southeast Asia would follow suit. The assassination of six pro-Suharto generals by Sukarno's supporters in the Indonesian Army led to counteraction from the right, pitting opposition parties, anti-communists, and conservative Muslims—including militant youth groups—against the Indonesian Communist Party (PKI) and its national apparatus, from the top down to the village level.

Terrifying beasts lurched through the land. Between a half million to a million men, women, and children were shot, decapitated with swords, or hacked to death with *parangs*. Many were accused and rounded up by gangs, then imprisoned without trial. Village forces, acting with the paramilitary *Komando Aksi*, executed in a systematic way, bringing thirty to fifty victims at a time to designated places, often riverbanks, to be slaughtered like cattle or goats during the night.[1]

It wasn't until many years later when I saw a documentary film, *The Look of Silence*,[2] that I realized the full horror of what had happened. The rivers of Indonesia flowed with blood, body parts, and the putrid remains of corpses—and a scourge of crickets sang without interruption about the deadly deeds. The forces of evil also killed thousands of Chinese, although many were businessmen and not PKI members at all. Few of them had allegiance to China or communism. The government created new discriminatory policies against those Chinese who remained in the country after this tragic year of bloodshed. As the documentary describes, most people remain silent about it to this day.

In the morning, Jamil and Jamsudin offered me a breakfast of egg curry with *roti*, a flat pan-fried bread. They seemed quite normal, with no signs of hostility or intentions to harm or rob me. I didn't know a lot about the situation in Jakarta, but I concluded there must still be active factions within the student population, and their pistols provided some sort of insurance.

For the next couple of days, I explored the city, staying out long enough in the evening to avoid being pressured to return to their brothel. I had a few meals in a modern hotel—a little too expensive for me—but I couldn't afford getting sick. Jakarta was a dingy, dirty, disorganized place. The water in its canals moved ever so slowly through cesspools of paper, plastic bags, feces, dead animals, offal, and oil. Millions of insects bred on the surface. Desperate people defecated, bathed, and drew water from whatever less clogged surfaces they could find.

I had to remind myself that there had been no orderly handover in Indonesia, as in the creation of Malaysia. The Indonesians had begun their fight for freedom from the Dutch in 1908, a low-level war that lasted until the Japanese invaded in 1942. The Dutch returned after the war but so did Indonesia's struggle for independence, which the rebels finally won in 1949.

In 1963, President Sukarno reasoned that the British aimed to continue their colonial empire when they fostered the creation of what he saw as a "puppet state," Malaysia. Sukarno launched an undeclared war between Indonesia and Malaysia, which was called *Konfrontasi*, the Confrontation. In 1964, Commonwealth troops from Britain, Australia, and New Zealand joined Malaysia's side. The three-year conflict entailed a series of border skirmishes, especially in Borneo where Indonesia held, and continues to hold, the largest chunk of land, Kalimantan. Along the border with East Malaysia, Indonesian troops infiltrated to stir up the local people of Sabah and Sarawak, who were, and remain today, much more diverse than the population of West Malaysia.[3]

In Sabah, a lot of action had taken place around Tawau, the small city near the Kalimantan border, which I had visited earlier that year to film volunteers. Although Malaysia and Indonesia achieved peace after Sukarno was toppled from power, a mild communist insurrection in Sarawak continued to fester. I had felt its indirect effects during my recent visit.

After three nights with Jamil and Jamsudin at the student hostel, I took a morning train to Yogyakarta in Central Java, a scenic ride that cleansed my mind of the grime of Jakarta. Luckily, my gut had not been hit by diarrhea—a fate that I had anticipated.

Rebecca, coming from Sarawak via Singapore to join me, flew into Yogyakarta airport. She was good-looking, cute actually, with short reddish hair and long legs—taller than most Indonesian men. She attracted a lot of attention but looked fit and able to take care of herself. It was considered unsafe for women—especially Western women—to travel alone in Indonesia. Many Indonesian men generalized from the behavior of female film stars in Hollywood movies and assumed Western women were loose and available.

We headed for our first destination, Mount Merapi, a name which means "the one that makes fire" in old Javanese. Merapi erupts, on average, every five years, according to records dating back to the 1500s. In fact, the last eruption had taken place five years before our visit, but we were told there would be signs if it wasn't safe enough for us to explore with a guide. Looking down from the top edge of the crater, the cauldron radiated much heat and stank like rotten eggs. The boiling orange pot and shooting streams of lava reminded me of the volatility of Indonesia. The killings in this part of Java had ended only a year before our visit.

After descending from the top of the crater, we took a taxi to the nearby ancient Buddhist temple complex of Borobudur, a giant hill of elaborately carved stone. We carried a tourist brochure, "Borobudur Temple Compounds," to understand the layout and history. The temple had been built during the eighth and ninth centuries C.E. when the Syailendra Dynasty was at its height, after Eastern Indian traders and missionaries brought Mahayana Buddhism to the island.[4]

The Empire was vast, and at one time the Bruneian kings in Borneo were vassals of Javanese kings. People had meditated and prayed at Borobudur for centuries until volcanic eruptions necessitated moving the seat of the empire. Gradually, the temple complex was covered by volcanic ash and then jungle, lost to memory with the coming of Islam in the 1500s. During their brief period of rule in the early 1800s, the British rediscovered the remains of Borobudur. Then the Dutch took over and completely unearthed it by 1835. At the time of our visit, the government of Indonesia was continuing the restoration work.

I had purchased some *ganja* from Jamil in Jakarta (one of his income-generating sidelines, I concluded) and had decided to bring it along for the excursion. Rebecca and I sat nearby and smoked some before entering.

If viewed from above, Borobudur looks like a huge *mandala* —a physical representation of the spiritual universe. For a couple of hours, we wandered in silence, feeling at peace. The stone reliefs spelled out the law of *karma*, the birth and life of Gautama Buddha, and his search for enlightenment. We progressed from *kamadhatu*, "the world of desires" to *rupadhatu*, "the world of forms," finally arriving at *arupadhatu*, "the formless world." I knew that The Buddha's final destination was the ocean of *nirvana*, a pure, liberated state, void of self; however, this was the first time I had experienced these ideas without the encumbrance of analytical thought. For a couple of hours, we floated, thankfully without a guide, meandering through the many statues and domed *stupas* until nearly sunset. Borobudur spoke to me of both the enlightenment and the power of a past era.

This experience brought Rebecca and me closer. We talked and laughed a lot, comparing our boring North American culture to this exotic place. We sat close together while taking a bus back to our hotel in Yogyakarta. We were both hungry and went out to eat and shop. It was then that I impulsively bought the batik painting at a local art store. It had caught my attention in a window display. I can't remember many more details about buying the painting, other than the fact that it moved me.

More than the painting moved me in that shop. Suddenly, I trembled with a different kind of "volcanic eruption." I had felt mild pings of pain during the day, but now the wicked beasts of gonorrhea came down upon me, a full-frontal attack. Rebecca and I were sharing the same hotel room. As we exited the shop,

I confessed my problem to her. She was really cool about it, kind of matter of fact. I took her back to the hotel in a *bechak*, and then asked the driver to take me to a clinic.

The Indonesian medical staff I met were equally cool. They knew the symptoms well—just jabbed me in the rear with a shot of penicillin and sold me a course of penicillin pills to take for the next 10 days. (This was before penicillin-resistant strains had developed and before the global HIV/AIDS and herpes epidemics, when love and sex were simpler. Ironically, I eventually became an international communication expert involved in convincing young people to avoid early or unprotected sex, especially with strangers—something I could do with experience.)

Contracting a sexual disease was a very depressing development for a sex-starved young man traveling with an attractive woman. Besides my need for abstinence, I knew Rebecca had another guy on her mind. But before my embarrassing situation arose, I was privately wondering if she might want to make love. I had really blown it. How stupid could I be? Fortunately, she didn't express any disgust, just laughed it off. I had to become Buddha-like and quell my passions—focus on talking and enjoying the architecture, art, people, and food of the land in which we were temporary guests.

From Yogyakarta, we traveled by train to Surabaya, took a bus to Ketapang, and boarded a quick ferry to Gilimanuk on the island of Bali. We rode on the back of a truck to Denpasar, where we stayed in a cheap guesthouse on the beach. We swam, walked, and talked, searching for sea shells. Our visit took place long before major hotel chains and package tours invaded Bali. Food was affordable and tasty, the people friendly and welcoming—no hustling or pressure to buy. It was a "take it or leave it" place: "Do join us, but please don't disrupt our way of life."

The appearance of the land belied what I later learned to be

Bali's turbulent history:[5] As in Borneo, early humanoid migration was followed by Austronesian peoples seeking its rich volcanic soils for rice and fruit trees, then Indian traders and missionaries and the establishment of Hindu and Buddhist kingdoms, the arrival of traders from China, and centuries of domination by the Javanese and Muslim sultanates. Next, in the early 1800s, and in quick succession, the Dutch alongside the French, then the British, followed by the Dutch again in 1816, who eventually consolidated their control over the whole Indonesian archipelago, including Bali. The Dutch fought local rulers under the pretext of controlling the smuggling of arms, opium, and slaves. Although Bali is known today as a land of peace and harmony, these battles were frequent and bloody. When the Japanese Army invaded in 1942, it carried out equally brutal occupation policies. Bali, along with the rest of Indonesia, was returned to Dutch control in 1945, at the end of the war. By then the people had suffered enough, and their anti-colonial struggle began anew.

Somehow, through all this political, cultural, and physical disruption, over 80 percent of the Balinese people remained faithful to the tenants of Hinduism. Was adherence to this religion their main strategy for survival, their counteraction to chaos? In the 1950s, they staged a non-violent campaign to resist new attempts at Islamization by Jakarta. They declared that their Hinduism is based on one central tenant, "*Om* is the essence of the all-prevailing, infinite, undivided one." This met the criteria of monotheism required by Indonesia's federal government and saved Bali from a new round of bloodshed. Unfortunately, the island had not been saved from the horror-filled, anti-communist killing spree during 1965–66.

Bali's violent history mirrored its many layers of soil from volcanic eruptions. At least twenty-five significant volcanoes were still active at the time of our visit. In 1963, Mount Agung erupted after a hundred years of slumber, destroying many villages and killing more than a thousand people.

Rebecca and I rented a motorcycle and ventured into the volcanic hinterland by day, visiting vibrant villages and Hindu temples, both old and new. People smiled and waved, including confidently bare-breasted women surrounded by multi-colored flowers and birds, palm trees, and ferns—visions evoking the Garden of Eden before the 'fall of man'. Children seemed to be everywhere, an overabundance of human fertility too.

We were reluctant to leave Bali when our time was up. We boarded a flight to Singapore. I was about to complete a large counter-clockwise circle of over 2,500 miles (4,023 km)—from Singapore to Jakarta, through Java to Bali, and back to Singapore again.

By the time we reached Singapore, I had also completed my course of penicillin and the beasts within me had been quelled. During that last night, Rebecca and I finally made love, the climax—so to speak—of a memorable, if somewhat frustrating, journey. I didn't know then, and never found out, what her motives were. Did she feel anything more than friendship for me? Had our relationship grown to the point where she was forgetting about the other guy? Afterwards, I felt that night may have been only a reward for my role as a good traveling companion—a pat on the back.

The next day, I boarded another flight to KK, and then traveled my usual route by motorcycle to Kota Belud. Rebecca had a shorter flight and bus ride to her post in Sarawak. In spite of my doubts about her, I already missed her a lot. Being so close to a woman on a similar wavelength and then returning to Kota Belud was an immediate downer. But I had to be realistic. She lived far away, and we had our assignments to finish. I had ambitions to make more films after Sabah; whereas, she didn't have any definite plans. She talked about going to Hong Kong for a while. I concluded we'd probably follow separate paths.

I WOKE UP in my comfortable chair in Kota Belud, the batik creation before me—its beasts and the blood they sought, the volcanoes and explosions of stars. The music had stopped, the record player needle returned to its resting place. My journey now seemed like a dream. My little bungalow was completely still. Eerie, actually. I imagined I could hear Peter's laughter.

I went to bed but couldn't sleep. I got up and put on my shorts and a shirt, slipped on my thongs, and walked up the road and around the corner, only to see the ghostly sheen of Caitie's empty bungalow, bathed in moonlight. I looked south towards the solid silhouette of Mount Kinabalu. I searched the horizon for the Southern Cross, but I was too far north. Other stars framed the mountain. A warm breeze from its direction touched my face. It was so silent—only the faint cheers of crickets and the muffled sound of *kerbau* munching on grass down the road.

I breathed deeply. I had come from chaos back to symmetry.

10

Blessing the Prodigal Son

10.1 My parents in Sabah

I'D BEEN GONE from home so long, I didn't know what to say. I'd been working on this visit from my parents for some months. For starters, I planned to put them up overnight in Peter's house in KK, where I was staying. But could they take such rugged conditions? From the airport's observation deck, I saw Russell and Alma McKee step onto the tarmac, sensibly dressed in tour-worthy light clothing, as I had advised in my letters. They made their way through immigration and to the baggage claim area, where I met them. I was suddenly dumbstruck. My parents seemed alien and out of place in my steamy, sleepy, new world. What would they think of it? After greeting them and grabbing Mom's luggage, I unconsciously reverted to Sabah English.

"You want to stay at same house I stay? Or you want to go to hotel?"

My mother laughed. "Neill, we can speak English. Why are you talking so slow and funny? Of course, we want to stay where you're staying."

I wondered if they thought I had become a little "touched" by all my exposure to the tropical sun. "OK, can-*bah*?" I stammered. "But very basic. A house on stilts. My friend Peter's place in a water village. Suburb of KK on the South China Sea. Peter's away on a trip."

"That sounds interesting," Mom offered in Dad's direction. Dad's silence indicated he was less convinced, but he played along.

I quizzed them about the first leg of their journey, a visit to Japan, where they had attended Expo '70, the world's fair in Osaka. A Japanese industrial bearing company had sponsored their stop in Japan because my father had, for many years, purchased this company's products for use in the manufacture of hay harvesters and snow blowers. My parents had always been interested in traveling and my father had taken trips to the UK and Ireland on business. When I was a teenager, he even made business trips to Germany and learned some German language. I was proud of all his achievements—and with only a grade eight education. I remembered him perusing the local *Kitchener-Waterloo Record* every evening and commenting on national and world affairs. I think that really influenced me.

I put my parents in a taxi and asked the driver to follow me on my motorcycle to *Kampong Ayer*, a water village consisting of over a hundred houses. At low tide, these simple, timber-frame structures stood about 10 feet above the South China Sea. The inhabitants were mostly rural-urban migrants, searching for improvements in living standards. On the one hand, nobody in the village paid land taxes since they were illegally squatting over government-owned shoreline. On the other hand, their presence was formally recognized because most of the residents paid for electricity and piped water supplied by the government. This was the kind of contradiction, or compromise, I had grown used to in Sabah.

I had anticipated correctly that my parents could maneuver the 200 feet (61 meters) of wooden walkway to Peter's house. This boardwalk had some flaws—a number of missing and loose boards—but they persevered. They had both turned 50 that year and were in good shape, but one mistake and they would have fallen into the water below. They had little chance of drowning at low tide, although they would have bathed in garbage: paper, plastic, rubber, bamboo, vegetable waste, and offal from hundreds of kitchens, as well as human and animal urine and feces.

The inhabitants of this water village simply squatted over holes in their floors to relieve themselves. The tide served as a twice-daily grand flush. At high tide, with cleaner water, the villagers took every opportunity to fish, while their children swam and played on the cross boards nailed to the piles below. I explained to my parents that the owner of Peter's house had built it solidly—and besides, I reported, on Sabah's coast there are no great storms or waves.

We had a clear view from Peter's house, no obstructions. I opened the windows to let them watch the sun set over the South China Sea, until lights from the night markets in the city center appeared across the bay.

My parents couldn't believe the world they had entered—people laughing and talking loudly, radios blaring all around them. I didn't want them to have to negotiate the walkway in the dark, so I

10.2 With Mom at Peter's house in Kampong Ayer

cooked them a meal of vegetables and rice with fresh fish—hopefully not caught from the water below us. I showed them how to use the hole in the floor for a toilet. They managed to squat, but with a great deal of difficulty, they reported.

I suggested we should all try to get some sleep because I knew the people in Kampong Ayer would rise early. I interjected the word "try" because I knew sleep would not come easily. Sleeping in such a dense settlement is a challenge because dogs howl and roosters crow throughout the night. Fortunately, our location was far from any mosque, so at least the early morning call to prayer was distant and muffled.

In the morning, my father looked pretty beat. He had always been a light sleeper and a bit of a worrywart. He was born on our family's pioneer farm, where chickens were kept at a respectable distance so that the crows of roosters would only be part of waking dreams. Likewise, hunting dogs were kept in pens and pet dogs slept in the summer kitchen by the old cast iron stove. Those dogs were taught their place with a good swift kick. To Dad, these Sabahan canines appeared to be ill-mannered, and "very mangy, to boot."

My parents had been teenagers during the Great Depression

in rural Ontario. Both had been raised in houses without indoor plumbing. Dad grew up with six brothers and two sisters, and Mom was a rural minister's daughter with nine siblings. Probably they didn't mind the fact that their son was experiencing some of the poverty they had known. As I made them coffee and French toast, a customary breakfast for me when I ate at home, I assured them they were going to love Kota Belud, which would be more comfortable and even familiar. I told them my bungalow was much like the cottages they used to rent for our family every summer on Georgian Bay.

I went to fetch a taxi and then returned to escort them once more over the walkway to the shore. As they carefully made their way back to solid land, the residents greeted them. My parents couldn't believe how friendly everyone was, even though they couldn't understand all that they said.

The taxi took them to the transport stand for Kota Belud while I followed on my motorcycle. At the stand, I negotiated their fare, asking the driver to drop them at Hu Hee Bit's restaurant, where I told them Rose would receive them and feed them well, in case I was delayed for any reason. I chose their transport, a sturdy new Land Rover, which took off in a flash. I stood there, picturing it going over the narrow highway and up through the hills, rolling through mountain passes, and careening around curves next to steep cliffs above the jungle.

Fortunately, or rather because I knew what could go wrong in Sabah, I had left a key to my house with Rose. On my way home, I had a breakdown, another flat tire. It took some backtracking to get it repaired, and I didn't reach Kota Belud until late afternoon. When I ran up the stairs to my bungalow, my parents appeared overjoyed to see me. Because of my delay, Dad had thought the worst, that I had gone over one of the cliffs. Mom told him not to be silly, that I had been driving that road for almost two years and was still alive. She reminded him of all the training he had imparted to me on the subjects of motion, machines, and mechanics.

I asked them, "Why are you inside? The view from the porch is wonderful and the evening is cool, the best time of day."

"Neill," my dad replied. "There is an awful stench out there."

I had lurched up the stairs and entered quickly, not noticing the rotten stink coming from under the veranda. I went out and peered downward to focus on the problem. I had been away for four days, and a stray dog had evidently lain down to die in this protected spot shortly after my departure. It had putrefied to such an extent that it was crawling with maggots.

I saw a group of male students passing by and called for assistance. In spite of their disgust, they complied. We borrowed shovels from neighbors, which the boys used to dig a shallow hole in the vacant lot next to my house. They somehow worked with one hand while covering their noses and mouths with handkerchiefs to avoid what they probably had been taught was "evil air," a vapor emitted from animal corpses. So much for Peter's and Kumar's science lessons, I chuckled to myself.

With a shovel, I managed to carry the corpse from under my porch for burial. I realized that help from my students for such a gruesome task demonstrated a real gesture of respect for me, and I thanked them profusely for their service. It never occurred to me to pay them. In Malaysia, I was their much-honored teacher. Any offer of a reward would have been completely out of place, a kind of insult and demonstration that "Mr. Nail" really didn't understand their culture after almost two years of living in Kota Belud.

Dad stood nearby with his camera, snapping photos of my students and me while we buried the dog. He was amused with the proceedings and chuckling at the way the boys held their handkerchiefs around their noses, like girls. I had grown used to the more effeminate side of male behavior in Malaysia from my first days in Kota Belud, when my new colleague held my hand while we

10.3 Burying the stray dog that died under my veranda

walked around town. This was a perfect introduction to local behavior for my parents...and an opportunity for me to discuss cultural differences with them.

I turned to Dad and said with a wink, "Welcome to Kota Belud!"

I had to teach that week, but I made sure my parents were well taken care of. They came to the school to meet my students, Mr. Kumar, and my colleagues. My friend Winston lent me his old car to take them around in the afternoons while he used my motorcycle. They walked around town looking at all the interesting provisions in the shops. Dad scratched his head and said, "Well I'll be..." when he saw that so many of the goods came from Communist China. Like most Western businessmen at the time, he had assumed that China was a "black hole" and manufactured nothing of value.

Other friends, such as the Singarasivams, a Tamil family from Ceylon (later renamed "Sri Lanka") entertained my parents. Dr. Sivam was the Kota Belud District veterinarian who told us he had escaped the growing tension between the majority Sinhalese and minority Tamils in his country to seek a better future for his family. He drove my parents all around to show them his agricultural projects: the breeding of an improved brand of cattle that did well in the tropics, experiments with new pasture, and up-to-date barn facilities. This was right up my dad's alley. His upbringing and business had been all about producing better animal fodder.

I wanted my parents to experience the life I lived in Kota Belud. They enjoyed a toned-down version of Indira Singarasivam's curries, which normally would blow your head off. They ate with me at Hu Hee Bit's restaurant, visited with Winston and family in their rustic house, mounted a *kerbau* held by a Kadazan man for a photo, attended the famous Kota Belud Sunday market, ventured over unpaved jungle roads in the interior, and visited a fishing village on the coast.

When the time came for me to take my parents back to KK for their flight, I put them up in a modest but comfortable Chinese hotel. In the morning, I walked them to a nearby Muslim restaurant and treated them to my favorite Malaysian breakfast, *murtabak*—a pan-fried, fine-layered, flaky bread laced with garlic, egg, and onion, and served with a piece of goat's meat in curry sauce. Good sports to the end, they seemed to enjoy what must have been an unusual breakfast for them.

At the airport waiting to board, we talked about some of the other surprises during their visit—the house on stilts over water, precarious roads, and the dog that had come to die under my porch—but most of all, the wonderful and welcoming people they had met. Then they boarded their plane for Hong Kong and flew on to Vancouver.

Reviewing old letters to my parents from Sabah many years later, I realized how important their visit had been to me. Out of a family of six, including four boys, I was the "Prodigal Son," the one who had left home and had forsaken a career in my father's footsteps. At one time, he wanted me to study engineering and join his company. But I had long ago decided not to take that route—any of my three brothers could do so, if that was their inclination and choice. My father never tried to dominate other people's decisions. I believe he realized I marched to the beat of a different drummer.

It had occurred to me during my parents' visit that I had inherited more of my mother's genes. I had been given her maiden name as my first name. At the age of 19, my grandfather Neill left Ontario for Evanston, Illinois, where he waited on tables to earn enough money to study at a Methodist Bible college. He met my grandmother in Cadott, Wisconsin, where he was a visiting preacher. They married and had five children in different small towns in Wisconsin, Iowa, Nebraska, and traveled as far west as Wyoming. They stayed in one place for less than two years. In 1907, my grandfather took his family with him back to Ontario, where they continued moving to new pastoral posts, all the while bringing five more children into the world. My grandparents lived in about twenty-five different parsonages before retirement. In other words, they "gathered no moss."

By coming to Sabah and sharing in my life for a week, my parents had blessed my chosen direction and honored my Malaysian friends. It had become evident to my mother that I was not going to become a Christian minister nor a missionary, as she would have preferred; however, it may have pleased her that I had ventured far from the comfortable and familiar, as her father had done. My two years in Sabah marked the beginning of many journeys to, and sojourns in, distant lands.

11

Rounding a Bend
in the Road

11.1 The road leading out of Kota Belud Valley

IN JANUARY 1970, Headmaster Kumar explained our new class schedule to the teaching staff. He spoke rapidly in his thick South Indian accent, referring to the chart he had drawn on the blackboard:

> The geography classes will be running parallel to the mathematics classes during alternative days except for the last week of the month so we will be adjusting the schedule to compensate for the extra holidays we are having in March and to be ensuring that the children all receive a good education which of course depends on your good selves, isn't it? But we will be

reassessing the situation periodically for we must be flexible and willing to compensate for the unknowable events, for you will be knowing that one, ha, ha, ha. But I am remaining optimistic that we will take every opportunity and have the best year even better than last year and as for physical education as you can see I am providing all possible opportunities to produce the best performance in fact beyond all expectations you can be sure for this is an important part of education as important as biology my own subject which I am continuing to teach to upper classes as indicated here. Are there any questions?

The staff members remained silent. Clearly, no one understood Kumar's class schedule, and his rambling explanation made it even less comprehensible. I looked over at Mr. Wahid, a teacher of Pakistani descent who spoke with a very proper British accent. Finally, he said, "But Mr. Kumar, there's a conflict in the classes I teach. Form 4 history is at the same time as Form 3 English on Mondays and Thursdays."

Kumar replied, "We will be making adjustments for that one."

"But when, Sir?"

"You are not to be worrying."

"But Mr. Kumar, what am I to do Monday morning when classes begin?"

Wahid's question suddenly unleashed pandemonium in the room. The usually silent and compliant Malaysian staff all spoke up at the same time, asking about their missing or conflicting classes. Kumar's management style disgusted us, as demonstrated in the previous year. We had learned a few days before, by Kumar's own proud announcement, that he had been confirmed as our permanent headmaster. Apparently, the Department of Education couldn't find anyone else with the proper credentials who would agree to be posted to Kota Belud. The authorities must have decided to go with the status quo, good enough for this difficult place.

Kumar, usually expressionless, looked somewhat shaken by the reaction of his staff. I figured, like the previous year, he'd spent little time on the schedule due to all the other pressures on him and, as usual, had made it up at the last moment. Now he was stuck. Finally, I raised my hand and said, "Can I offer a suggestion?"

Kumar, looking for any avenue to salvation, replied, "Mr. Neill, of course you can be offering. We are having an open process here."

I walked up to the blackboard and began to erase his schedule. The room fell silent as I continued. When I'd completely wiped it away, I carefully drew the schedule I had prepared. It required all the boards in the room, so it took some time. Some of my colleagues chatted, some remained silent, possibly watching for a reaction from Kumar. I knew my action was bold, but I also understood that, as the only foreigner on staff, I had a certain amount of idiosyncrasy credit. Malaysian teachers couldn't afford to get on the wrong side of Kumar. Making someone lose face is normally something to be avoided in Asia, because the transgressor will never be forgiven. For them, Kumar's retribution could have boomeranged in unpredictable forms at any time, possibly months or even years later at some other school. With my remaining short time in Sabah, I had little vested interest.

When I finally completed chalking out the schedule, I turned to Mr. Kumar and my colleagues and asked, "Are there any questions?" For a moment, everyone remained still, and then Wahid began to clap. Next, all the others joined in, and the pace of their applause increased.

Kumar quickly jumped up to take advantage of the moment, uttering his famous phrase, "ThatiswhatIsaid! Very good improvements to my plan, Mr. Neill."

And so, began my temporary job as the unofficial deputy headmaster. Kumar started to rely on me to help make major decisions and solve some problems. I had come to know him pretty well and was sure that it was impossible to make him the complete fool since he could bend any reality to his advantage, at least in his mind. Although he had converted to Islam to shore up his standing in Sabah and receive a permanent appointment, I felt he remained a Hindu at heart. In one of his past lives, in some previous manifestation, time, and place, he probably had written my version of the schedule on a blackboard.

As the school term began, I took over the duty of fostering the first Form 4 class in Kota Belud. They were working towards the Form 5 exams, the approximate equivalent of Grade 11 or 12 in Canada and the US, or what they then called "O-Levels" in Britain. I remained focused on English and Geography while ensururing these students would receive the best attention possible in other subjects.

Kumar and other teachers stepped in to try to cover the holes left in mathematics and science with the departure of Peter. I was also thankful for our colleague Edward, who gave a lot of support. He was a Tamil and a Christian but not really religious. A good friend, I could talk to him with ease. We shared a sense of humor. I still needed someone with whom I could frankly discuss some puzzling aspects of Malaysian culture.

Edward demonstrated some fear about living and working in Kota Belud, due to its reputation. I helped by talking him through some of his anxiety. I think, in retrospect, most of his unease was based on racial prejudice. Although Edward was not particularly dark for someone of South Indian origin, in the view of at least the older generations of Chinese and native people, he was still a *keling*, which meant "black person," a term with a derogatory connotation. Despite appearances, official tolerance, and the ubiquitous Malaysian motto "Unity in Diversity," this kind of racism still ran deep in Malaysian society, at the time.

I understood the theory behind affirmative action for the native people of Malaysia. Indeed, I was part of the movement to advance their education. But some volunteers felt we were only providing cheap labor, holding posts, and blocking the advancement of Chinese and Indian Malaysians until natives could take our places. There seemed to be something intrinsically unfair in the system, but I could do little about it and had to take the long-term view. In any case, the *Bahasa Melayu* syllabus, an officially approved formal Malay language education system, would soon be introduced in lower secondary grades in Sabah's government system. It would replace the English syllabus in less than a decade. In the future, teachers would have to perform in the national language, and native Malayic language speakers would have an advantage.

In February of 1970, I attended a meeting in Miri, Sarawak, for all CUSO volunteers in East Malaysia. We discussed weighty issues such as the low allowance we received from the Malaysian government—a third of the salary earned by a Malaysian teacher doing the same job. Unlike Peace Corps volunteers, who received their pay from the American government, CUSO's policy involved host governments paying as much as possible to ensure that they solidly supported the presence of Canadian workers in their country. We were not Canadian government employees, although Canada's federal government gave grants to CUSO for volunteer recruitment, administration, orientation, placement, and repatriation costs. In Malaysia, CUSO had been topping up the Malaysian government allowance with an additional amount, which brought our income up to about half of a local teacher's take-home pay. This was still considered too little by those who wanted the Malaysian government to appreciate them as "counterparts" rather than as "volunteers."

Volunteers from the first such service in the country, Britain's Voluntary Service Overseas (VSO), were paid the same amount from the Malaysian government as we were paid. The idea of volunteering was clearly written into the name of their organization. We weren't individually recruited or contracted by the Federal Government of Malaysia or by the Sabah government. They clearly saw us as a different category of adventure-seeking "do-gooders" who wanted to contribute something to their country. The allowances they gave us were no secret because we had to go to government pay offices to collect our monthly stipend, which, in my case, involved signing on a big ledger, clearly visible to others. When some locals saw or heard how little we were paid, they thought we were being cheated. A person's earnings are an important part of his or her status in Malaysia, more so than in North America. Few locals could understand why we would give up two years of a larger salary in our home countries to work for a pittance in theirs.

At the meeting in Miri, many volunteers wanted to vote for a closure of the program. I was not in favor of this motion. I was learning so much about the world. Who could dispute the other benefits to me and to Canada, so long as I put my new knowledge and experience to good purposes? Quite frankly, I was more interested in distributing the latest minutes of our NBFS's fantasy meetings and in recruiting new members.

In addition, my skills in basic Malay were comparatively better than others, mainly due to my posting in Kota Belud, where the townsfolk spoke little English. I had been teaching Shakespeare, and I amused my fellow Canadians by giving a speech in Malay, actually a literal Malay translation of Marc Anthony's famous piece of oratory in which he ironically praises Brutus for killing Caesar. It brought a much-needed moment of comic relief to our heavy proceedings. I amused myself by thinking, if we closed down the program, when would another Canadian ever have a chance to make such a speech?

In spite of my trepidation on returning from vacation in Indonesia, the last eight months in Kota Belud were probably my most productive. I fully immersed myself in the challenges of my job and the life of the town. The rhythm of long days of teaching made time pass quickly. I convened Form 4 students for extra afternoon classes in an older building near the town center. My words were often drummed out by the pounding of four o'clock rains on the metal roof.

I became very close to my small group of Bajau, Kadazan, and Chinese senior students. I thought some of them would become important people in Sabah, and this mentoring became my appointed task and last act in Kota Belud. The idea of leaving before they took their Form 5 exams bothered me. My two years would be finished in August, and their exams would not be held until the end of the following year.

I learned through the KK volunteer community that a new group of CUSO volunteers would arrive in August and that not one of them was due to be posted to Kota Belud. I talked this over with Kumar, for we had learned to work together, and I found him to be quite reasonable when not under too much pressure. I asked his blessing for my plan to go to KK to see the Department of Education on the matter. I got hold of the list of volunteers coming

11.2 Some of my Form 4 students at Kota Belud, 1970

and found a suitable couple: he taught science and mathematics and she taught English and general subjects.

I made an appointment with Mrs. Chin, a sympathetic ear in the department who was in charge of volunteer placements, and I lobbied hard for this couple's posting to Kota Belud. I argued that since the Peace Corps teachers had gone, and with no replacements in the foreseeable future, these Canadians were the only hope for my students. I told Mrs. Chin I was leaving in August. I had not completely made up my mind before this meeting but decided that if I stayed for even three more months, the couple wouldn't be posted to our school. It would then suffer a shortage of qualified teaching staff the following year.

When I told my Form 4 students I was leaving in August, they were very disappointed. The girls cried. Their sad eyes said, "How could you abandon us?" I told them I was pretty sure they would be getting at least one new Canadian teacher. I didn't want to say too much more about the expected replacements because I knew someone else could lobby hard and divert them from Kota Belud. I gave as much reassurance as possible, while thinking to myself, if all else fails, I could probably stay for three more months until a solution could be found.

During these last few months, I spent some weekends and one school break in KK at Peter's place, editing and producing my film. He owned a 16mm film viewer plus cutting and splicing equipment. The conditions in his house in *Kampong Ayer* were not the best for editing, and my project budget didn't include a "work print"—a copy of the camera original film for cutting and joining different shots in various sequences, viewing each montage, and then making more revisions—so I had to very carefully handle the original to avoid scratches and damage. During those visits, I also finished writing the script, timed all the sequences by putting the film through a projector, and recorded the voice-over track at Radio Sabah. For no charge, they also mixed in Sabahan and other music, storing the soundtrack on a quarter-inch tape.

I chose the title *Manu Ulu?*, a phrase meaning "Where's the backwoods?" I intended this title as an ironic reflection on the fact that most would find East Malaysia relatively modern, compared to first expectations, but I'm not sure anyone ever understood the title without my explanation.

I couldn't completely synchronize the picture and sound, but with no on-camera interviews it didn't matter too much. I played the finished film in KK for Canadian volunteers—not a great thing to do since putting the camera-original through a projector contributed more scratches. I simply needed affirmation that the film would pass their inspection.

When I screened it for them, I also invited the Deputy Director of Education, a sympathetic man. At the end of the showing, he came up to me with some issues. In the narration, I had asked questions that brought him some discomfort: "Should we be here? Should we be supporting a government that favors the advancement of some ethnic groups over others?" His concerns surprised me a little since he was Chinese Malaysian. Perhaps I was being naïve. He had to protect his position and the future presence of volunteer teachers in Sabah. He asked me not to show the film again in Malaysia, if possible.

At least my Canadian colleagues really liked *Mana Ulu?* and so I decided to let it go as it was and not do any more revisions. That could be done in Canada later, I thought. I wanted to send the film back to Ottawa with a proposal to do more CUSO recruitment films and photography. This prospect provided a good deal of my motivation for finding replacement teachers. I hoped to get on with a career in filmmaking, a plan which seemed a good bet for me. I loved it. I had a pretty good eye with the camera and a good sense of sequencing. But my work had flaws, as I discovered after the fact: not enough variation in shots, too few close-ups, and too many long sequences. In fact, I had a lot to learn.

On top of that, I didn't know at the time that my old Bolex camera, when set at the normal 24 frames per second, was actually running slightly faster. This made all the action appear slower when projected, but fortunately not full slow-motion. (This wasn't an issue for Peter's film because it was more expressionistic and experimental. He called it "Möbius Strip"—a joined, continuous band. I think of it now as a personal statement that he never finished—perhaps the ironic point of the title.) I don't think my Canadian and Sabahan previewers noticed the slight slow motion because it matched our slower pace of life in Sabah, where people took "time to stop and stare," as the Welsh poet, William Henry Davies, wrote in his poem, "Leisure," bemoaning a time when Western life was at the pace we experienced in Sabah.

In mid-August, the new Canadian couple, Paul and Evelyn Gervan, arrived in Kota Belud. I overlapped with them for a few days. They took over my house, and I sold them my old Norton motorcycle. Such overlaps are not always appreciated by newcomers. Although some prefer to find their own way, these people appreciated my efforts to introduce them to everyone I knew and to provide a basic orientation. They were attractive, I thought, with style—wearing flower-patterned tops and bellbottom jeans. In a way, I was a little jealous of the social access they would have as a couple. Their experience, I thought, would be very different from mine. They loved the whole setup—the bungalow, the students, their colleagues, and the school, as well as the people in the community they met. I stayed for the first day of school to see my Form 4 students relax. "Mr. Nail" had come through, as promised.

After a final supper at Hu's *kedai*, I walked with the newcomers back up the hill to our house, teaching them how to avoid cow pies in the dark. They went to bed and I sat on the veranda to watch the valley bathed in moonlight for a last time—my favorite place on earth.

In the morning, I boarded a Land Rover with a small bag containing some clothes, my camera, and my edited film. Other travelers joined. The driver loaded and tied their luggage on the roof rack, which soon bulged to a dangerous level. One lady climbed aboard with a rattan container, which held her three prize chickens for sale.

As our overloaded vehicle chugged its winding way up the long hill out of Kota Belud Valley, I kept looking back at the place that had so changed me. I wondered if I would ever return. Rounding a bend in the road, I looked over my shoulder one last time as my North Borneo home disappeared from sight.

12

The Sabah Situation

12.1 My fiancée, Beth Diemer, in Japan, 1971

"You don't understand the Sabah situation!" Matt shouted, his eyes and Adam's apple bulging as he slammed his fist on my desk. "There's going to be a war here, a rebellion! We have to be ready! I'm digging a tunnel from my house to the airport!"

"Don't you think that's a bit of an overreaction?" I offered.

"No way, man. It's coming. The revolution's coming, and we have to get ready! The Kadazans and the Chinese are going to rise up." I smiled as he continued, "You're not taking this seriously, man. It's real serious. You're supposed to be our leader. Can't you do your job?"

As Matt went on and on, my thoughts wandered back to the peace of Kota Belud. It had been only two-and-a-half years since I'd left Sabah in 1970, and now I was back—posted to KK as the deputy director of CUSO in Malaysia. As such, I had to look after the welfare of almost thirty volunteers. The numbers in Sabah had really swelled by February 1973. My job also involved travel to Sarawak and West Malaysia, supporting volunteers, and finding new placements for vocational teachers, teacher trainers, foresters, geologists, engineers, social workers, and others.

By the time I came back to Sabah for this second two-year stint, about a dozen Canadian volunteers lived in KK, too close together—like a Canadian enclave. Many of them were housed in the pleasant suburb called "Tanjung Aru," near the airport. Rumors flew around. Anything I said might come back to me in a distorted form, sometimes weeks later. The situation was actually a bit of a shock to me.

Matt left the office, exasperated and muttering expletives. A few minutes later, Jeff entered with an intense and spooky look in his eyes. As he approached my desk, he stated, "I need new glasses."

"What happened?" I asked.

"I lost them on the road to Tamparuli. But it was a good experience. I was on my motorcycle, and suddenly I saw Christ rising out of the jungle...I threw them away." Jeff said this in a manner which indicated he was most pleased with his revelation and salvation.

"Well, did Christ tell you that you wouldn't need your glasses anymore?"

"I was so inspired."

"But your new vision didn't last?"

"I see the world differently now."

"But you still need glasses? Did you look for them?"

"It was dark and the bushes were very thick. Now, I really don't know where it was on the road."

I had to smile, picturing an orangutan trying them on with greater appreciation than Jeff. I finally relented, "OK, Sophie will give you a letter for the optometrist on the next block. We have an account with him. But I have to look up the policy. You will probably have to pay back CUSO."

"Why would I have to?" Jeff asked.

"Well, you threw them away."

"But I was inspired!"

"Sure. Section 14b in the policy manual on religious inspiration," I mumbled to myself.

"Are you doubting my experience? I saw Christ. He's going to save the Kadazans!"

While Jeff glared at me, I wondered if he and Matt needed professional counseling for their delusions. Perhaps they smoked too much *ganja*. I figured Matt and Jeff used it a good deal when they weren't teaching. During my time as a volunteer, I had occasionally smoked pot with other foreign volunteers, but always in moderation so it wouldn't affect my job. I had identified some heavy users in this new group. Before going to school each morning, one guy sat on a rock in the sea, eating his porridge, waiting for the right cosmic harmony to begin his day, while the local community watched in amusement from shore.

When Jeff left, I lay back in my chair and looked at Sophie, my Kadazan secretary. I could see her trying to keep a straight face. She had mothered these people before my arrival, perhaps a bit too much. Was she a part of the rumor mill?

I went out for a walk along the seawall to get some air. Had I done the right thing in coming back to Sabah? Had things changed so much so quickly that I now didn't understand "the Sabah situation"? What was I doing here? I looked northwards over the South China Sea.

MY THOUGHTS DRIFTED to the time I had left Sabah in August 1970. I'd landed in Hong Kong, where I bought a new still camera and a Super 8 movie camera—blowing a good deal of my repatriation money. I hoped to have a new filmmaking career ahead of me and was in no hurry to settle down. Before I left, Peter had become engaged to an attractive Anglo-Indian girl, Arlene. After their wedding, they planned to leave Sabah so he could start graduate school. Before departing, I'd also received a letter from my senior high school girlfriend, Ruth, reporting that she'd met a British guy, a Peace activist, while traveling in the U.K. She was engaged to be married. Ruth and I had stayed in touch by mail. At one time, I suggested that she come to Sabah to stay with me. I didn't write anything about getting married—my lack of commitment continued. In truth, it was a dumb idea since I would have been too busy teaching and filmmaking. She probably sensed that I wasn't too serious, just a bit lonely.

From Hong Kong, I flew on to Tokyo to have a film lab make a copy of *Mana Ulu?* with a soundtrack. I sent it back to CUSO in Ottawa, along with my proposal to do more filming in Asia and Africa on my way home. I had confidence that it would all work out. I couldn't afford to fly home if they didn't give me the job, but teaching English in Japan would be my alternative. Such jobs were easy to get back then.

Caitie had taken a job teaching English in Kyoto, Japan. She connected me with a friend of hers, an American Lutheran volunteer staying in a hostel with other Lutherans near Shibuya Station in Tokyo. They taught English in Japanese schools and did other jobs, trying to promote understanding between the US and Japan—no proselytizing or preaching. I found the residents at the hostel very friendly. They allowed me to stay free of charge, so long as I contributed to the groceries, cooking, and chores. One of them had donated a stash of marijuana.

One evening when we were somewhat stoned, a new volunteer arrived from the US. Her name was Elizabeth Diemer, but everyone called her "Beth." She wore a leather band across her forehead, like an Indian princess. She smiled and seemed to glow. She was even more radiant when I met her in the kitchen for breakfast. I couldn't take my eyes off her.

Her parents had named Beth after Princess Elizabeth of Britain. Beth was born in New Guinea, where her father continued to serve as an American Lutheran missionary. She'd spent a good deal of her life there and in Australia, as well as part of her childhood and university days in Iowa. I found her to be a blend of Asia-Pacific and North America cultures, spontaneous and expressive. Sparks of attraction immediately flew between us.

During the following week, when she didn't have Japanese language class, we spent much time together at the Canadian Embassy's National Film Board theater. I showed her my new film before sending it to Ottawa, and we watched documentaries. We even had our own projectionist on standby, but no popcorn. I couldn't afford to take her to movie theaters. We talked a lot and went "Dutch treat" to coffee and noodle shops.

Although I had been in Tokyo a couple of weeks, I knew next to nothing about Japanese culture, so we explored together. People stared at us a lot, unlike in Malaysia. I found that unnerving. Once when Beth was at language school, a man stopped in the street, pointed at me and shouted in my face: "Hiroshima! Hiroshima! Hiroshima!" I didn't know what to say. It was 25 years after the Americans dropped the uranium fission bomb nicknamed "Little Boy" on that city. Being a Canadian, I thought I had nothing to do with it. I remained silent and nervously shrugged, since I doubted he spoke any English. Japanese culture was even more insular than it is today. To him, I represented another ugly *gaijin*, a foreign invader.

Beth had to go to her teaching job in a Japanese school north of Tokyo, in Urawa Ward, Saitama Prefecture. I decided to hitchhike around Japan while waiting for an answer from Ottawa about doing more filming. I headed north to Hokkaido and then down the western coast. I stayed in *ryokans*, Japanese inns where I slept in large rooms next to male and female strangers on *tatami* mat floors. I used public baths where naked women could easily be seen on the female side from joint entrances. This openness, I thought, contrasted sharply with the otherwise extreme politeness and formality of the Japanese. I had no problem getting rides because almost all Japanese who had learned a smattering of English wanted to practice their language skills. This usually led to a few exchanges in English, and then a lot of gestures and attempts by me to use the few Japanese words I had picked up.

Next, I traveled to Kyoto to see Caitie. On meeting, we immediately began to recount stories and laugh about our times in Kota Belud. We had so much in common in that regard. Caitie showed me around some temples and shrines, and we drank tea and ate in Japanese restaurants. Kyoto was then, and remains today, a cultural center of Japan. I loved its sights and sounds, a sacred place. All this spirituality contrasted with my memories of the stories I'd heard concerning the atrocious slaughter by the Japanese Army in Malaya and Borneo during World War II. My American friends told me that there was a Japanese proverb, "When you are away from home, there is no reason to be ashamed." I thought this explained a lot, if it was true. I also wondered if this was the reason I saw so many drunk men in business suits at train stations, many too wasted to walk.

I took a train to Nagasaki, the city where the Americans dropped the second nuclear bomb on August 9, 1945, only three days after the first one fell on Hiroshima. This one was a plutonium-core fission bomb nicknamed "Fat Man." It was obvious the Americans wanted to experiment with their different weapons. The Japanese military didn't even have the time to assess the damage from the first bomb and had not yet surrendered, a very formal process that involved telling the Emperor the real truth about the war they had lost. In Nagasaki, I climbed a hill overlooking the rebuilt city, now sprawled out along Nagasaki Bay. Here, I had an experience that compensated for my shock of the man yelling at me on the Tokyo street—a rare moment of inter-culture communication:

As I snapped some photos from the hill, a tour guide handed me a pamphlet. Each page revealed blackened rubble, sizzled skin, and stunned panic. I felt nauseated and had to turn away to focus on tall shipyard cranes—like exclamations against a setting sun. The guide's girlfriend, dressed in a *kimono*, looked at me and joked with him in Japanese, her dark eyes reflecting the new white buildings rising around the bay below us.

Suddenly, a pigeon landed on a ledge near us. "Pigeon, symbol of peace," the guide said in heavily accented English.

Snapping the bird's photo, I repeated, "Yes, symbol of peace."

She poked his side and snickered in Japanese, "Clever fellow, *gaijin* understood."

I smiled too, guessing at what she said.

On my return to Tokyo, I found the letter from Ottawa. It was a go! I was ecstatic. As requested by me, they also included a bank draft for a new 16mm movie camera with a zoom lens, a tripod, tape recorder, and lots of film and tape stock, which I would purchase in Hong Kong.

I wanted to meet Beth and tell her the good news. I also felt I needed personal time with her alone, since I'd misunderstood something she'd said during our last meeting. She had just ended a close relationship with a Lebanese guy before she left the US, and she was adjusting to that separation. I had some doubts about

whether she really cared for me. We had spent so little time together, so naturally we gave off some mixed signals. My feelings
for her deepened through this brief meeting. I wanted to spend
more time with her, but, sadly, we had to say goodbye, promising
to write. We made no commitments to one another. I flew off to
Hong Kong, and then on to Thailand, to begin my new career. But
Beth and I carried on as pen pals. I told her about my adventures,
including the women I met.

In December 1970, after completing coverage of Thailand and
during my filming in India, I took a break and traveled by bus over
the mountains to Kathmandu, Nepal. After checking into a local
hotel in the early evening and venturing onto the cold streets, I
entered a place called "Café Eden," where travelers were listening
to '60s music and exchanging views on where to stay and what
to eat. Hashish tea and shared pipes of hashish accentuated the
music. Next came hashish brownies. In a very short time, I became totally stoned. Instead of feeling harmony, I started to feel
completely cut off from others in the café. Their eyes seemed to
detach and float, staring at me.

I escaped to the street. A small, half-frozen beggar boy came
up to me, but I was in no condition to help him. It was I who
needed help. I retreated to my hotel. The walls of my second floor
room closed in on me—dangers all around—my jackknife, my
razor, the window I could open. Doors along the corridor shut
tight, people talking and laughing inside. I escaped to the cold
and shadowy streets again, echoes of their laughter in my head.

While I stood frozen and shivering against a wall, I heard a
greeting from a stranger with an American accent and I turned
to see a middle-aged man in a business suit emerging from a shop
door. He could see I was in distress and asked if he could help. He
escorted me back to Café Eden to talk things through, shielding
me from those glaring eyes. I asked him not to leave me alone
that night, so he took me to his hotel room—surprisingly, right

beside mine. He ensured that I drank plenty of water to clear my system, and I lay on a rug on his floor.

My panic gradually subsided as we traded stories about living in Asia. When I told him that I'd been teaching in Sabah, he talked about viewing Borneo on flights between Vietnam and Australia. Was he with the military or American intelligence? I didn't ask. He also told me of an incident in his life. Once attacked by a tall, threatening street thief, he threw a rock and hit the man between the eyes. He may have killed him but never stayed to find out. It sounded like a confession. As he related this story, I saw David and Goliath, Vietnam, and my home in North Borneo as fractured thoughts, all connecting in rapid fire imagery. Finally, exhausted, I fell asleep on the floor.

In the morning, my head had cleared somewhat. The American made sure that I ate a full breakfast before he said goodbye and good luck. I never wrote down his name and address and, to this day, have no idea who he was—the good Samaritan, David, and the CIA? My trinity in one.

By this point in my travels, having known Peter, Caitie, Tom, Beth, and many others from the US, most of my Canadian-born, self-righteous, anti-American sentiment had dissolved. This man washed the residue away. If my one and only experience with LSD in Sabah had been heavenly, this episode with hashish was like a descent into hell. Somehow, I regained enough mental strength to carry on with my filming job, although, at first, the loneliness and paranoia frequently returned. It took many years for these feelings to clear my system completely. They kept coming back, especially in times of stress.

From India, I traveled to East and Southern Africa—Ethiopia, Kenya, Tanzania, Malawi, Zambia—and then on to Nigeria in West Africa. I filmed and photographed numerous CUSO workers in a variety of situations. It took me until March 1971 to reach Canada and begin producing my new films.

CUSO arranged for me to work at Crawley Films, an independent film studio in Ottawa. The best thing that happened to me during this period was my work with and guidance from Sally MacDonald, an older woman who was one of the first female graduate engineers from the University of Toronto. Instead of going into engineering, she became a superb film editor at Crawley's. She had screened my footage as it came in from overseas before I met her. She made a lot of notes on how I could improve, which CUSO sent to me during my travels: more close ups, cutaways, different angles, fewer long shots and zooms.

I must confess that CUSO never used my funny first film made in Sabah, *Mana Ulu?* Besides the slight slow motion, it was slow-paced, with some long, boring sequences and a preachy tone in places. Fortunately, the Director of Information, Iain Thomson, a "Geordie" from Newcastle, England, had a great sense of humor. He must have recognized my potential talent. Iain had worked for newsreel services in Australia and England and knew something about production "on the fly." Perhaps I impressed him by the way I was able to produce *Mana Ulu?* with so few resources and in such conditions.

I worked with Sally day after day, editing sequences and absorbing her critique of my shooting and edits of sequences. This is when I really started to become a filmmaker. Our partnership led to the creation of two good films. And CUSO wanted more!

On the return leg of a filming trip to New Guinea and Malaysia in November 1971, I stopped in Japan to stay with Beth for six days. She had first lived with a Japanese family in Urawa Ward, really improving her language skills. But she had recently moved to nearby Omiya Ward, where she rented a miniscule apartment. Her bedding, placed on the *tatami* floor, had to be put away each morning for lack of space.

I saw her in action in her community. She spoke and acted like a Japanese woman, although she claimed, modestly, that she

12.2 With fiancée, Beth Diemer, November 1971

could only speak at a child's level. I admired her rapidly learned grasp of a complicated language and culture. She was not only lovely, she was open to new experiences and new ideas. She also had integrity and possessed the core values that I knew I needed to help steer me through life. Although, at the time, she remained a solid Lutheran, she had studied comparative religion at the University of Iowa and was quite open to other religious thought and experiences.

Beth was no prude, and our love-making was great. Near the end of that week, I asked her, "Will you join me in Africa on my filming trip in April?"

She, thinking the school year would be over in April and her time in Japan was due to end in August, at any rate, replied, "Sure, I'll marry you!"

In total, we had spent less than three weeks together; and yet, this seemed like an OK idea to me. But there was a problem. A woman I'd been dating in Ottawa had already moved into my apartment. Somehow, I had to get out of that relationship to be with Beth. I knew after the week with her, I'd been kidding myself about my feelings for this other woman. Telling her about Beth was one of the toughest things I've ever done.

In April 1972, without the usual fanfare of a wedding gift registry, reception plans, venue reservations, tux rentals, bridesmaid dresses, or a rehearsal, Beth flew from Tokyo to Lusaka, Zambia, where I was shooting another film for CUSO. In fact, Beth had created a wedding invitation with her own calligraphy, printed it, and had sent out three hundred copies before she left Japan. She titled it "An Invitation to Dance." We were pretty sure no one would come from her side or mine—too far and expensive. But one great American couple did arrive, Dick and Jeannine Helmstetter, one of two *gaijin* couples in Beth's Japanese home city. Dick, an amazing young man, had put himself through university playing snooker and making elaborate pool cue sets that all the professionals wanted. Some American investors backed him to start a billiards cue stick and table manufacturing business in Japan. He wrote off the trip to Zambia as a search for exotic hardwoods for his business.

Dick and Jeannine were witnesses to our marriage at the Office of the Registrar in Lusaka, where the Zambian government official asked, "Will you, Nelly McKee, take this woman to be your husband?"

This question was in keeping with our confusing joint marriage proposal and I replied, "Yes, definitely!"

It all turned out well in the end. As usual, I had little money, but Dick and Jeannine paid for our wedding dinner for ten at the Ridgeway Hotel in Lusaka, inviting three other Canadian couples. Jeannine made the arrangements. She was a great social "mover and shaker" who could step into any situation and politely put it right. (Her father had been on the Manhattan Project, the US government venture which designed and created the nuclear bombs

President Truman had decided to drop on Japan to end the war. Through her work in Japan, Jeannine became so much loved by the Japanese people that a portion of her ashes was eventually buried in a special shrine in Kyoto.) With such people blessing our wedding, we felt no need for a church or minister.

As newlyweds, Beth and I traveled through Zambia, Botswana, Tanzania, and Uganda, while I completed my filming and she created pencil sketches. We returned to Canada, where Beth met my family and friends for the first time. We rented an apartment near Ottawa's little Chinatown. Beth learned to cook Chinese dishes, improve her Japanese culinary repertoire, and ran our household, all the while practicing her oriental calligraphy.

Once again, I edited my films at Crawley's, but by the end of 1972, CUSO had enough recruitment films. I wrote some film proposals and sent them to different international development agencies. None of them was accepted.

With no other films on the immediate horizon, when the deputy job in Malaysia became available, I applied for the post and got it. I agonized about this because I felt I really should continue with filmmaking. When I told Sally—now a good friend—that I was returning to Malaysia with Beth, I felt a little like a deserter. But she understood—a married man with responsibilities. She knew the struggle I'd face in trying to break into the Canadian film scene with neither credentials nor reputation, except in CUSO. Like most industries, filmmaking depended on who you knew as much as what you knew.

So, STANDING at that KK seawall in February 1973, I shifted back to my new "Sabah situation." A lot had happened to me. I believed that I could now more wisely interact with Matt, Jeff, and other heavy *ganja* users, due to my many experiences around the world—including that "bad trip" in Nepal. But like the American stranger in Kathmandu, I avoided preaching abstinence. Besides, it would have made me even more unpopular and "uncool." It was the 70s, after all.

Fortunately, on my return, I worked closely with the CUSO Director, Peter Hoffman, who was based in KL. Due to my reputation as a volunteer and filmmaker, Peter made a special effort to recruit me. We had met in 1971 when I was shooting a film in New Guinea, where he was, at the time, the deputy director of CUSO. He and his wife, Barbara, had both served as volunteers in Sarawak before getting married. They talked about the great times they had there, as I did about my first stint in Sabah. (Coincidentally, Barbara was the same entertaining and motivating returned volunteer whom I had met and respected during orientation in Vancouver in 1968. I replaced her as deputy in Malaysia when she became pregnant and couldn't travel any longer.)

At first, I couldn't easily comprehend why some of our more recent volunteer recruits to Sabah didn't value their time in this relatively easy place. Given my experiences in visiting and filming volunteers enduring tough situations in India and Africa, I found it hard to understand some of the KK crowd. I had photographed and filmed CUSO nurses helping desperately poor people in Indian hospitals, the chaos of Nigeria right after the Biafran War, agronomists advising on crops and food storage in drought-stricken Northern Ghana, and a CUSO couple scraping green stuff off cow's liver before cooking and eating it in their tiny *rondavel* in Botswana.

When Beth and I arrived in Sabah in February 1973, we made a tour of the western side of the state. This included a return to Kota Belud to introduce Beth and see some of my remaining students and colleagues, old friends in the community, and Paul and Evelyn, who had succeeded me and who so much enjoyed the place they had extended for a third year. We shared the same philosophy—just do a good job of teaching, enjoy life, and ignore all the politics some volunteers seem to be fixated on.

Beth spent her time in KK running our household and learning how to cook Malaysian and Indian dishes. She rode her bicycle to town to visit the British Council Library and shop; and otherwise, she spent most of her time on her calligraphy. I admired Beth's resourcefulness and watched her development as an artist. She had studied Japanese calligraphy in Japan. In Malaysia, she spent many hours learning Chinese calligraphy, studying under the best teacher in the country when we went to the capital of Malaysia, KL. Eventually, occidental calligraphy and artistic bookmaking became her life's vocation.

Beth was not an employee of CUSO. She indicated early in our stay that she had little interest in spending all her time with Canadians—a frank and spontaneous utterance that spread like wildfire. Beth didn't understand her role as the wife of a field staff, but she eventually grew into it. In a way, she had made a declaration of female independence which was not understood by some of the volunteers, including women.

Matt, who had declared I didn't understand the Sabah situation, and Jeff, who had thrown away his glasses, posed only the beginning of my problems. One woman, stoned most of the time, ran off with a traveler to Bali, leaving behind her husband and three-year-old daughter. Another loved being pursued by a local politician, who got her pregnant. I helped her arrange an abortion and an early departure. Still another was raped, and I spent hours counseling her. One guy suffered from culture shock and loneliness, and I had to talk things through with him to determine if he had the strength to return to his isolated post. I also had to mediate a conflict between a volunteer and his Malaysian supervisor who, when I met him, appeared to be "shaking in his sandals" at the thought of further contact with his angry and demanding Canadian employee.

Around mid-1973, the Regional Director arrived from Bang-kok. Famous for his interest in peaceful resolution to problems, he practiced a Quaker-like approach with a deep belief in egali-tarianism. We called him "Mahatma." He talked to me and to the unhappy volunteers and then counseled me on listening more. This was a bit of a blow, since I had always thought of myself as a good listener, beginning in my younger days as a budding psychologist in Calgary. He asked me to move my desk against the wall so that I wouldn't interact with people across a physical barrier. This was a good suggestion, I thought, but probably just window dressing on deeper problems in the recruitment process. I began to have self-doubts and started to hate my job. I thought about quitting.

My own experience as a volunteer teacher in Kota Belud did not seem to count much among many of these strangers in this familiar land. Some of them had gained professional experience in their fields before coming to Sabah. To them, I was just a young filmmaker and former volunteer with little relevant experience in the administration of development programs. To some extent, they were right, but that's how CUSO functioned—with little bureaucracy. Its decision-makers were willing to take chances on people.

More important, from my perspective, was that some of the volunteers didn't appear to appreciate the country they lived in— the cultures, flora and fauna—riches I saw all around me. They didn't breathe the same fragrant air. My experiences belonged to me alone; their minds were like alien boxes. Waking dreams began my daily struggle with reality. I asked myself, in which di-rection should I move? Where do I belong?

Then, Bill McNeill, the CUSO Director of Overseas Oper-ations, arrived from Ottawa on a familiarization tour. He had worked in Nigeria in rough-and-tumble times. He didn't suffer fools gladly. After meetings with some of the KK crowd, including our most dissatisfied volunteer and his boss, he promptly ordered a ticket to send this guy home.

Bill stayed at our house, arriving with a bottle of whiskey. He recounted his adventures in Africa and told us about some of the political battles in CUSO Ottawa. He treated me like an adult and even asked if I wanted a field staff job in another country or a job in Ottawa after this stint. That night when I went to bed, I slept deeply for the first time in many weeks. I had been drowning and suddenly surfaced for air. By Bill's action, a signal was sent out to all the other discontents that their continued tenure had conditions. If they didn't enjoy their life and work in Sabah, they didn't need to stay.

I also felt my mental balance restored by our contact with local residents during this second stint. Beth and I lived quite frugally in a small apartment, without hot water or aircon, in Teck Guan Villa, a suburb of KK. Each morning we were awakened at around five by the cooing of Jambu Fruit Doves as a prelude to songs of the White-rumped Shama, followed by Oriental Magpie Robin melodies.

It's not that we had chosen to live in the jungle. Our downstairs neighbor, Robert Yap Theng Hong, liked to keep these exotic birds in cages. He remained oblivious to their shrill calls in the early morning. The Yaps were Hakka Chinese who talked in very loud voices, the tones penetrating our louvered windows, picking up where the birds left off.

The word "Hakka" means "guest families," indicating migration. They are Han Chinese but, unlike others, are not named after any geographical region or city in China. In Sabah, Hakka are the largest ethnic Chinese group. They are responsible for a great amount of the state's economic development through logging; establishing and operating plantations of tobacco, rubber, coconut, and oil palm; as well as running traditional businesses, such as shops and restaurants.

Robert, an auto mechanic, was one of the first to be trained by Toyota in Japan. His wife, Celia, spent her time raising their family, which eventually grew to five daughters and one son. We became close enough to attend family weddings and funerals. We helped the whole family migrate to Canada, where they fully integrated into the Canadian tapestry—four of their children married Canadians of European descent—and the Yaps became our friends for life.

By the time we came to Sabah, my Peace Corps housemate from Kota Belud days, Peter, had married Arlene and left for graduate school. Arlene's parents missed them a great deal. Jimmy and Francie were from Bangalore, India. When we first had them over for a meal, they critiqued Beth's Indian cooking, instructing her on how to improve her skills. Jimmy made special *chapati* pans for us out of cast iron. *Chapati* is Indian flat bread. There are many ways to spell it but only one way to cook it, according to Jimmy and Francie. Going forward, Beth stuck to cooking non-Indian foods for them. This interaction uncovered a real, and refreshingly frank, cultural difference. In fact, I have found that many Asians will tell you quite bluntly, but in an affectionate and instructive way, how you have failed in interpreting their culture and how to improve.

We also got to know a Kadazan civil servant, Monggo Orrow, and his expressive Greek-Australian wife, Zoe. He was one of the people I related to in the Sabah government—very level-headed. He helped guide me in dealing with some of our personnel problems regarding "the Sabah situation." Zoe, on the other hand, had no patience for such people. Her arms would flail as she talked, mimicking the airplanes needed to send them far away.

Our friendships with these people were soon replicated in relationships with some of the new volunteers we helped to select, orient, and place. Derek and Elizabeth Hamlet were a couple who assisted me with my greatest need of all, comic relief. Derek became the NBFS's East Coast correspondent under the pen name of "Sir John Trepan Cozenage." They were posted to teach in Semporna, that isolated place I had visited and filmed in 1969.

Derek contributed to new NBFS newsletters, warning of an impending doom due to Orcish tendencies still running through some elements of the population of Sabah, including Canadians. Their first daughter, Nicole, was born in the rudimentary Semporna hospital where feral dogs ran through the wards. I helped save her through an emergency flight to KK for the blood transfusions needed after a premature birth. Elizabeth required an injection with a special serum because of the Rh blood factor— complicated issues, all handled well in KK at its Queen Elizabeth Hospital. The Hamlets were made of strong stuff, and they renewed my faith in our mission.

Regardless, by the end of our stay in Sabah, we decided to gradually phase out the education program and focus only on a few technical positions. The Hoffmans and I agonized over this decision because we had enjoyed such life-changing experiences as teachers in Malaysia. Eventually, I concluded that some of the KK volunteers had expected more difficult conditions and challenges and had become disappointed because they thought they were merely supporting a budding middle class. I didn't have the power to recreate my own volunteer experience in others.

By the time we packed up to leave, I understood that "the Sabah situation" was really inside your head—or your heart. One person's paradise was another person's swamp.

13

Serendipity

13.1 The haunted Fairwinds Hotel, Port Dickson, West Malaysia

SERENDIPITY HAS ALWAYS PLAYED a great part in my life: my rooming with Wasfi Youssef from Egypt in university days; my posting in Kota Belud, where I met Peter with his movie camera; my friendship with Caitie and the connection to her friend in Tokyo, leading to my meeting Beth. I never planned or calculated my life's course. It's been rather like a series of lucky happenings—timely opportunities, friendships, and lasting relationships.

One time, on a visit to Singapore during my first stint in Sabah, I entered the main post office to mail a letter to my parents. I looked down the counter to see Douglas Edenborough, a guy I went to school with who lived less than a block from us in my Canadian hometown of Elmira. While making a backpacker's trip around the globe, Doug had just happened to stop at the same time and place to mail his letter home as well.

When I returned to Malaysia in 1973, I learned that John Soehner, also from Elmira, had joined CUSO as a teacher in Bentong, Pahang, West Malaysia. As children, John and I had started school together and played together. He had attended my birthday parties, and we were in the same senior class in high school. But we had lost touch. Did our similar backgrounds lead us to do the same thing in this same faraway country? We never really settled that. By then I'd come to understand that, above all, serendipity reigns.

During this second stint in Malaysia, Beth and I spent at least a third of our time in West Malaysia, often staying with the Hoffmans, who were open and friendly to us and to all the Malaysian volunteers. They always had visitors.

I helped to recruit, place, and support volunteers. I ran the whole program when Peter and Barbara went on home leave. During my most difficult times in Sabah, these retreats to the West were true escapes from "the Shadow of Mordor," as I jestingly called it. Another task involved running orientations for newly arrived volunteers, imparting our knowledge and experiences alongside that of Malaysian experts.

Some of the orientations took place in Port Dickson, at the Fairwinds Hotel, an old edifice on a hill overlooking the Straits of Malacca—a two-story affair with concrete arches and Roman columns grown over with moss. A Chinese tin mining millionaire had built it as his seaside residence in the early part of the twentieth century.

As the story goes, the Japanese military police took over the Fairwinds during World War II for use as an interrogation center. They tortured many people inside the rooms where we slept, and they chopped off numerous heads on the grounds outside. Then, after the Japanese surrendered, the former owner reclaimed his property, only to have his son commit suicide by jumping from the cliff in front of the house and smashing into the rocks next to the water below. Possessed by a *hantu*? Of course.

Ghost stories are one of Malaysia's specialties, possibly because of the confluence of so many oral cultural traditions. There are reports of over eighty haunted hotels in the country. Mr. Lim, who ran the Fairwinds, never told newcomers outright about the Japanese history. Bad for business! Stories floated amongst guests, regardless—most definitely part of the attraction—at least for foreigners. New guests might start to hear or imagine things: a door that wouldn't stay closed, strange knocking on the walls, groaning sounds in the middle of the night. We could easily visualize what had happened in this building 30 years earlier. These stories added a little more spice to our orientation sessions, alongside Mr. Lim's fish head curries, and none of our trainees ever jumped off the cliff, that I can recall.

We also brought interesting characters to our orientations to give new volunteers a good overview of Malaysia and to educate them more broadly on Southeast Asia. This included discussions on the causes of the election riots of 1969 and the rationale behind the New Economic Policy, the government's affirmative action program that gave preference to the *bumiputera*—the Malays and other indigenous peoples.

We exposed our trainees to speakers from the Chinese and Indian communities. For example, the Malayali-Malaysian journalist M. G. G. Pillai rendered entertaining anecdotes about politics and ethnic issues, including the discrimination experienced by the Indian community. During his career, Pillai gave his perspectives in a no-holds-barred style of reporting and commentary. Although he had many brushes with Malaysian authorities, politicians' doors remained open to him.

By exposing new recruits to such informed people, we tried to prepare them to keep open minds and not to completely side with any particular ethnic group in Malaysian society. As temporary guests, that was not our role.

Michael Morrow, an American journalist based in the region, also broadened our horizons. He had traveled to Taiwan after graduation from university in the US. Instead of returning home to answer the call of his draft board, he stayed in Asia. During the war in Vietnam, he spent a lot of time in Hong Kong and Saigon and helped to set up the Dispatch News Service, which broke some of the major stories of the war, including the infamous My Lai Massacre.

Michael had been captured and held by the Khmer Rouge in Cambodia for about 40 days. He talked his way to freedom due to his intense and honest personality, his facility with Asian languages, and his strong stance against the American war, which had spread to Laos and Cambodia. Michael had been expelled from South Vietnam because of these opinions, but he continued to work in the region, based in Singapore at the time I got to know him.

Our diverse guest speakers gave new volunteers an overview of the regional political and economic context in which they worked. Most young Canadians, like Americans, were against the Vietnam War, and by this time Canada had given shelter to about thirty thousand draft dodgers. During the same period, an equal number of Canadians had joined US forces to fight in Indochina, and Canadian industries profited through their contributions to the American war.

We carefully recruited and placed new volunteers—a lesson learned in Sabah. We also interviewed prospective supervisors and then matched job descriptions with the personal profiles and backgrounds of new recruits. For instance, Bill Dumont, a graduate forester from British Columbia, tried to bring some sense to Malaysia's forest industry by introducing inventory methods to regulate the harvest of rapidly disappearing hardwoods, thus helping to strengthen replanting initiatives. Bill charged through the jungle with his *parang*, clearing the way to see the real picture. Bill's Malaysian counterparts only came up to his shoulders. He had confidence beyond his years and experience; and yet, he displayed sensitivity to local culture and maintained a realistic attitude on the changes he could help to achieve during his brief tenure in Malaysia.

Memories of those days in the 1970s are like the Chinese dish called "sweet and sour pork." We visited volunteer William Howard in Alor Setar, West Malaysia, a traditional Muslim town located in the northwest of the Malayan Peninsula. He worked for the government as a drainage and irrigation engineer. After meeting him at his workplace during the day, Beth and I joined him and a friend in the evening. They traveled all around town on their motorcycles to various Chinese restaurants, while we followed in our car. He called it a "pork crawl." In one *kedai*, we started with pieces of quick-fried pork and vegetables. We ordered only one dish at a time, moving on to five or six places in all, gradually spiraling downward to pigs' feet and pigs' ears, all washed down with beer.

Eventually, William upped the challenge, ordering slices of pig's snout in which holes for chopsticks had been provided by the animal's natural anatomy. At our final stop, using his fingers in the shape of a sack, William motioned to the *towkay* to bring an order of pig's testicles, a dish that I couldn't face. I gladly let him win the contest.

That evening was the sweet part of this memory. The sour part came a few weeks after I had finished this second stint in Malaysia. I received a message that William had been riding his motorcycle without a helmet. Involved in an accident, he had fallen onto the pavement and died of massive brain injury. In spite of the frivolous tone of his revelry with us that evening, he was a young man with great social, diplomatic, and technical potential who never had a chance to continue a promising career. Once again, my own luck in life came to mind on hearing about William, for the motorcycle helmet I wore as a volunteer in Sabah, although embellished with whimsically protective Elvish script, was a very flimsy affair.

Canadian volunteers usually took two-year assignments. One of the most interesting short-term postings we made was Russell Johnson, a 75-year-old hardwood sawmill expert from Northern Ontario. We sent him into the West Malaysian highlands to help the *Orang Asli* (aboriginals) set up and operate a sawmill donated by the Canadian government. He had retired and was seeking adventure and relief from boredom. His wife, Maud, wanted to stay put in Sault St. Marie. He already had been to East Africa on a similar mission. Surprisingly, I don't think Africa was quite as tough as the highlands of West Malaysia, where he spent over a month.

The *Orang Asli* are Proto-Malays—Austronesians who arrived thousands of years before the Malays. It's not really known, but they probably came to the Malayan Peninsula around the same time as the Kadazans, Muruts, Ibans, and Dayaks reached Borneo. When the Malays arrived, they killed or captured many *Orang Asli* as slaves and drove others deep into the highland jungles. Like the story of aboriginals all over the world, they remain near the bottom of the economic ladder in Malaysia. Enter Russell Johnston and the sawmill.

I arrived at Russell's highland station one cold and drizzly evening. After talking with him for some time, I learned he was making slow progress. All sorts of bureaucratic impediments had been placed in his way. He also looked a bit gaunt, so I enquired what was ailing him.

Russell answered, "Well, you see, Neill, I haven't eaten much in days. I feel kind of weak, actually."

"What's the problem?"

"Well, the food ain't so good. In fact, it's pretty godawful."

"What are they feeding you?"

"Same old thing, day after day. Some rice and a few fried vegetables and some meat that's hard to chew. I think I'm losing weight."

I grew concerned. "No variation at all?"

"No, in fact the lady, or maybe it's a man, not sure, who brings me the food never changes the rice."

"What do you mean?"

"Well, it comes to me cold and the first time it came I wasn't hungry enough to eat much. I just took a few spoonfuls off the top. Then it came back the next day with the same spoon marks. I knew the dents I made. I thought that it was queer but then, by golly, if it didn't come back three days in a row. Same bowl of rice!"

"That's awful," I sympathized. Just then, the cook came in with drinks. Right away, I figured she was an *Orang Asli* transgender person. I asked her a few questions and quickly established the problem. She spoke little English, so Russell couldn't complain directly and he didn't want to offend—a good Canadian. I decided to take Russell back with me to KL to restore his health and negotiate with the *Orang Asli* administration for better food and support for his mission.

We had a great week with Russell as a guest. He gained weight and we gained many stories on his work in the Northern Ontario bushland and in Africa. He went back to the highlands to complete his mission successfully, taking along a carton of food in case he had to face more bowls of stale and dented rice.

Although Beth and I returned to Sabah to pack, we spent the last few months of 1974 and January 1975 in KL. Peter and

Barbara departed, and I took over as acting director until the new director would arrive. We nearly always had company. Volunteers dropped in to stay overnight. But we didn't mind. The Hoffmans left us a grandmotherly Malay *amah* (maid) by the name of Lina, who did the cleaning and cooking while Beth concentrated on her Chinese calligraphy. Lina laughed with us a lot—one of the most cheerful persons I have ever met. Nothing could fluster her.

I had begun to investigate my next move. I wasn't keen on continuing as a field staff, managing people. I wanted more creative work. My two-year sojourn as a volunteer teacher in Kota Belud had led me to an awakening of mind and soul. From there I had launched my new career of filmmaking, which—after my experience with "the Sabah situation"—was the road I wanted to travel on again. During my second sojourn in Malaysia, I had been allowed to bring CUSO's filming equipment with me and had taken a trip to Bangladesh and Laos to document some projects for Ottawa. I also completed a film on volunteer foresters in West Malaysia. My mind cleared, and my focus improved when handling the camera or working in an editing studio. I started to explore what I could do if I based myself in the region, perhaps linked to people like Michael Morrow, the journalist.

In December 1974, Beth became pregnant with our first child. I knew I had to chart a plan with some kind of economic security. Considering this and seeing no clear way forward in filmmaking, I became a bit depressed. Luckily, on one of his visits, Michael got me into jogging to build up my body and confidence, and I pulled out of the funk. He had married a Vietnamese woman and was living on a shoestring budget as a freelance writer and publisher, so anything was possible, I thought.

Then, like some kind of angelic messenger, a friend from Ottawa, Clyde Sanger, arrived in KL. We knew each other from CUSO meetings, and he had seen some of my films. He was working for the International Development Research Centre (IDRC), a public corporation based in Ottawa. He told me that his organization needed someone to make films and do photography and that I should look him up when I returned to Canada. After he left, I wrote him, asking for the job.

Three months later, on a snowy March day in 1975, I walked into the offices of IDRC, where I didn't even have to make a formal application. There, I met with Clyde and talked to a few other friendly people. I don't recall filling out any forms—my letter to him had sufficed. The next day, Clyde handed me a letter of appointment as the organization's filmmaker and photographer. Serendipity reigned again!

14

Paradise Lost

14.1 A view of Sabah as it once was

OUR HELICOPTER FLEW low over the treetops as I put my right
foot on the step, leaning outwards for better camera angles, but
firmly buckled in to avoid a catastrophe. I looked for a stretch of
unbroken jungle and motioned to the pilot to head south, away
from the Kinabatangan River. I could see that there wasn't much
left of Sabah's rainforest in this area. He complied, and after 20
minutes, we finally reached a stretch of forest where I managed
to get some decent sequences.

It was March 1987. I'd been working for IDRC since March
1975. Now I was shooting a film on rattan, a palm species which

creeps up tall trees in tropical forests. Rattan is used to make furniture, handicrafts, musical instruments, shelter, food, and medicines. I already completed filming on Hainan Island in Southern China. This would be the last of many documentary films I had made, and my second chance to return to Sabah on assignment. I had visited Sabah briefly in 1979 to take some sequences for a film on tropical oyster culture.

During the previous 12 years, I'd traveled several hundred thousand miles to over fifty countries, filming the results of research on new methods of forestry, agriculture, fisheries and aquaculture, low-cost housing, education and community development, health delivery systems, as well as, water and sanitation. My job served me as a continuing university course on current issues in human development, while Beth happily stayed in Ottawa developing her occidental calligraphy skills and network.

For much of this time, I acted as a one-man crew, sometimes hiring sound technicians and editors. I enjoyed researching and writing the shooting scripts, doing the camera work, and recording interviews myself. After completing the rattan filming, my plans were to take Beth and our two young children, Derek and Ruth (born in Ottawa in the mid-70s), to Tallahassee, Florida, where I would do a Master's Degree in Communication—a sabbatical year sponsored by IDRC.

I had started as a filmmaker in Sabah, so it was a fitting closure to this part of my career to see North Borneo once again through a camera lens. On this 1987 trip, I had traveled by speedboat from Sandakan to the Batu Putih forestry station on the Kinabatangan River, where I completed the technical sequences, such as nursery operations and harvesting. The river had recently flooded, killing off a good deal of the rattan plantations near its bank, so it was very difficult to get any good shots from a boat.

The Kinabatangan River Basin is the original home to thousands of species of fauna and flora, a cradle of biodiversity, but I

14. 2, 14.3 Filming oyster culture in Sabah, 1979

wasn't really prepared for what I saw from above. Recent floods presented growing evidence of the ongoing over-logging and burning of all vegetation that remained, a scorched-earth method used to prepare land for plantations. The resulting soil erosion, floods, and loss of forest cover spelled disaster for local inhabitants—and for our global climate.

When I first arrived in Sabah about two decades earlier, primary tropical forest covered 80 percent of the land. At that time, the Murut, the last people in Sabah to renounce headhunting, still inhabited the deep jungle in the interior, living in longhouses. Until the early part of the twentieth century, a Murut man had to show at least one human victim's head to his potential in-laws before winning a bride.

For thousands of years, the Kinabatangan and its tributaries had served as the Muruts' lifelines and highways. They practiced "shifting cultivation" of hill *padi* and tapioca, which involved moving their crops to new land whenever the soil became depleted and needed to lie fallow to be restored. For protein, they fished and hunted wild boar and barking deer, using blowpipes with poisoned darts.

For centuries, Borneo's forests attracted Chinese traders in search of the main ingredients of bird's nest soup—Swiftlets' nests made from their own saliva, and found in caves. The traders also sought resins, rattan, beeswax, nuts, and animal trophies such as elephant tusks, rhinoceroses' horns, and hornbill casques. Except for these non-renewable animal products, throughout the years, traders had exhibited a certain respect for the sanctity of the forest, the source of all of these riches.

I could see no remaining signs of that respect as I looked down from the helicopter. I had seen such destruction in many other parts of the world during my filming trips. Some call it economic development. I call it politics and greed. I remembered the rumors that had floated in the '60s and early '70s about people receiving logging rights to tracts of forest in exchange for supporting certain politicians in power. Some people converted to Islam as a prerequisite for acquiring these concessions.

This struggle for power and money, and a lack of coordination between environmentalists and legislators, has spelled disaster for the majestic hardwoods of Borneo such as meranti, the slow-growing ironman tree, and the aromatic agarwood, known as "wood of the gods" because it is used in the construction of Asian temples. Most recently, much of Borneo's forests have been cleared to make room for plantations of oil palm, the fleshy fruit of which is squeezed to make an oil for cooking and food production, as well as an ingredient in many other products, including soap and cosmetics.

While the cultivation of oil palm and the development of tourism are both considered by key planners to be strong answers for the economic development of Sabah, the two strategies clash because of the unregulated exploitation and destruction of primal forests, which tourists come to see. The effect on the island's ecology is devastating—the heart of Borneo is being torn out.

As our helicopter headed back to Sandakan, we flew over the lowland forests closest to the coast. The rapid discharge of water, due to inland forest exploitation, causes floods in vast stretches of this area every year. But the Kinabatangan floodplain also serves as protection against the onslaught of human activity. Its excess water saves the forest in this area from aggressive harvesting and provides a home for saltwater crocodiles, monkeys, orangutans, and a few remaining elephants.

Along the seacoast, mangrove forests—a nursery for many species of fish and shellfish—still remained in place. These coastal forests and those along the rivers of Sabah are also the home of the proboscis monkey, the mature male member of the species known for its large flopping nose and huge pot belly. For me, the Kinabatangan floodplain and mangroves provided a glimmer of hope in an otherwise depressing scene.

We landed in Sandakan, a place I had always found somewhat mysterious, way off on the East Coast of Sabah. Sandakan is where the American author, Agnes Keith, wrote her memoirs, *Land Below the Wind* and *Three Came Home*, before and after Japanese occupation. Sandakan had gained a reputation as a "little Hong Kong," a Chinese city on the edge of the Sulu Sea.

In the Suluk language, the name "Sandakan" quite fittingly means "the place that was pawned." An arms smuggler from Glasgow, William Clarke Cowie, established the first European settlement on Sandakan Bay around 1870. Some unknown force, perhaps hired pirates, promptly burned it down. In 1872, the Sultan of Sulu granted a German by the name of "Schuck" an area of land along Sandakan Bay to set up a trading post for rattan. The rattan business likely provided a cover for more nefarious trading activities in arms, opium, slaves, and just about everything else that flowed through those pirate-infested waters at the time.[1]

I was also interested in the effects of so-called economic development on Borneo's animals, so I stopped to visit the Orangutan Rehabilitation Centre in Sepilok, a few miles outside the city. This center had been opened in 1964 to rescue orphaned orangutans from illegal hunting, capture, and trading, as well as from the destruction of their habitat by logging and plantation activity. The sanctuary is composed of about 10,000 acres (4,047 hectares), most of which is virgin rainforest. The orangutans are fed and nurtured here in an environment that gradually builds their confidence and skills to return to the jungle for the rest of their lives. Fortunately, they are not fussy eaters. They are considered "frugivores" or fruit eaters, but they will also eat young leaves, flowers, bark, and insects such as ants, termites, pupae, and crickets.

I amused myself by looking for the glasses that the Canadian volunteer, Jeff, had thrown away in 1973 when he claimed to have seen Christ rising out of the jungle. I had always imagined them to be on the face of a more appreciative orangutan. I didn't find his glasses, but I met an older and somewhat cranky female orangutan who had been given the name of "Susan." She apparently had decided to hang around and help her human counterparts foster others of her kind. She exhibited hostility towards white humans of the female gender and had been known to bite them, or so I was told. We got along fine and even shook hands.

I couldn't think of how to work these fellow hominoids into my film story since rattan has a prickly bark, making it very difficult for use by orangutans or people to take Tarzan-like swings through the jungle. But the vines, once stripped of their bark, make great swinging chairs, a luxury Susan preferred, at any rate, and I took a shot of that.

In Sandakan, I boarded a plane to KK, where I rented a car to drive to Kota Belud. The town seemed much the same, though with a few new shops and government buildings. I stopped to

14.4 My former bungalow in a sorry state

14.5, 14.6 Goh Eng Kian and family posing in front of their house

look at my little bungalow on the hillside and found it somewhat rundown. I didn't knock on the door. At least I knew no foreign volunteers stayed there, since I'd heard all such programs had closed in Sabah. I visited the secondary school where I had taught, now surrounded by trees and other plants, unlike the barren plain we had inhabited when I first arrived in Sabah in 1968. I greeted the native headmaster and explained that I'd taught in his school 17 years earlier. He didn't seem interested, which I at first found strange. But then, what else could I have expected? The whole curriculum had been converted from English to *Bahasa Melayu* and probably few people remembered our era at all.

I made the rounds of former students I could locate, all married with children. This included Goh Eng Kian, the "Mr. Fixit" of my volunteer days. He had a transport business and a substantial modern house. Born into a relatively poor family, his high school education really advanced his position in life.

Hu Hee Bit, the *towkay* who owned the restaurant where I ate, had died some years before. I met his son, still operating the place, and got the address of his sister, Rose, in KK.

I found Mrs. Sing still living in the same house across from the Muslim cemetery. Her husband had died, but she appeared to be in good spirits while she told me all about her children and grandchildren. I learned my old friend, Winston, her son-in-law, was teaching in Tuaran, a town not far off the road to KK.

I drove there and tracked him down. He had graying sideburns but otherwise looked and acted like the same "Asian cowboy" I had known back in my Kota Belud days. We went to a coffee shop to catch up on what had happened during my absence. Winston wanted to hear what I was up to.

"So, you make films, man, all over the world. Very good-*bah!* Lucky you got out of this place. Sabah's very *sempit-bah,* narrow place."

"But you're doing well as a teacher. Got a promotion, no?"

"A teacher? I hate it. Stupid job, stupid system-*bah!* But I'm out of here soon."

"Where are you going?"

"A logging concession is coming through, man. Big one. I've got a friend in government."

"That's very good." I responded without enthusiasm, thinking of all the destruction I had recently witnessed. I didn't probe further as to what he had to do to gain such a prize, and I didn't want to know. I thought it best to leave my memory of Winston as it was, the perpetual gambler, dreamer, and schemer who loved people. I shifted the remainder of our short discussion to talk about our families—superficial "catch-up." He told me that his children had all grown up and he was now a grandfather. His youngest was still in secondary school, and the others were in different occupations. His wife enjoyed good health. I told him my parents, whom he had met, were still alive and healthy. I talked about Beth and her artwork and the fact that we had two bright kids.

I drove to KK to get my onward flight. I also took a chance and drove into town to find Rose Hu. She was working in a general provision shop in the heart of the city. She had finally married an older Chinese man, the shopkeeper, and never had any children. She seemed destined to live out her life selling goods and catering to his needs. No better opportunity had come along since that British soldier had jilted her in the early '60s.

As with Winston, our meeting depressed me a bit. Rose acted very reserved, maybe because she thought her in-laws would think I was that Brit, the source of all the former gossip. I didn't really know if that gossip had been passed on to them, but I decided to mind my own business in the future.

I left the shop and walked to the seawall to view Gaya Island, the original West Coast settlement of the British North Borneo Company. In 1897, the famous Mat Salleh, a terrorist or freedom fighter (depending on your point of view) burned the place down, including the administrative office, which had to be rebuilt on the mainland. The British finally killed him, but it appeared to me that his descendants got their revenge. Compared to the early 1970s, I noticed a big increase in the percentage of Malayic people in Muslim dress on the streets.

That trend had begun under Tun Mustapha, the Chief Minister in the 1960s. He was a Suluk-Bajau, born in a *kampong* near Kudat on one of two peninsulas that jut out like animal ears into the Sulu Sea, pointing northeast towards the Philippines. Many in Sabah were of the opinion that Tun Mustapha wanted to flood the land with his people and drive up the numbers of Muslims in the population.

These new arrivals are called "Moros" in the Philippines, due to that country's colonization by Spain, which itself had once been occupied for centuries by the Moors from North Africa. These illegal immigrants to Sabah came mainly from the Sulu Archipelago and Mindanao, many fleeing war and repression by their Catholic-dominated government in Manila. Most of this migration had been gradual and without conflict—people following their kin in search of better opportunities. Compared to life in the Philippines, the relative affluence of Malaysia, with its Muslim-dominated government, was attractive.

The Malaysian and Sabah governments had done little to stop this influx of migrants, with the result that squatter settlements had sprouted up in many places. The influx of these poorer people led to the destruction of some coastal forests and mangroves— uncontrolled tree cutting, overfishing, and pollution. According to Malaysian authorities, crime rates, including drug trafficking and piracy, had greatly increased. In 1985, Moro pirates attacked the East Coast town of Lahad Datu. At least twenty-one people were killed and eleven injured, and this was only a portent of things to come.[2]

So, I thought, maybe what the volunteer, Matt, claimed in 1973 had been correct, after all. I didn't fully appreciate the coming "Sabah situation." How could he have divined this future? Did the *ganja* help? When I flew out of KK that day in 1987, I realized that the paradise I had known as a young man had already been lost. I concluded that the often-quoted saying, taken from the title of the book by Tom Wolfe, was right: "You can't go home again."

15

You Can Go
Home Again

15.1 Scene on Jalan Ranau Bypass near Kota Belud, December 31, 2005

AFTER MY DISAPPOINTING RETURN to Sabah in 1987, I had resolved never to go back again—better to just retain my fond memories of the place when I lived there. But I didn't understand the
real meaning in the title of Tom Wolfe's novel until later. It's about
an author who depicts his hometown in a bad light and is driven
out. He's disgusted with his place of origin and America, itself,

so he travels the world and sees the upheaval in pre-war Europe, with Hitler on the rise. He returns to America with new respect for his country and the town he came from.

In 2005, while we were living in Moscow, Russia, where I was working for Johns Hopkins University on youth health, a chance arose to return to Sabah. One day, Beth went to Indonesia's Independence Day celebration at that country's embassy, where she bought a bunch of raffle tickets and embarrassingly won many prizes because the organizers didn't shake the bowl properly. One prize was a return trip to Jakarta on Indonesia's Garuda Airlines. Beth asked the Guruda ticket office whether the plane stopped in Kuala Lumpur, Malaysia, and if she could get off there. They gave her a green light, so I purchased a second ticket.

We arrived in KL on December 26, 2005. By then, the city had become a booming metropolis, not the relatively sleepy city we had known in the '70s. After taking a subway and monorail ride, we found our way to Jalan Ampang, a street where we had lived and worked during various periods in 1973 and 1974. We found it difficult to identify landmarks but managed to find our old office on the second floor of a building—the same dental clinic located below. I flagged down a taxi driven by a friendly Malay fellow who agreed to take us on a search for our past haunts. We started with Bok House. During our time in KL, it had been occupied by a French restaurant, then known as *Le Coq d'Or* (in Chinese, people pronounced it "Lee Kok Do"). But by the time of our visit, it was surrounded by high-rise office buildings and department stores.

Our driver told us that the old house was haunted, and the authorities had not yet been able to evict the *hantu*, still dwelling within. Bok House had many rooms, including one that was rumored to have once been used as an opium den. However, I believe that the real problem was a conflict between conservationists, the government, and some other parties who wanted to make millions on new real estate development on that land. Sadly,

15.2 Bok House, Kuala Lumpur, December 2005

a year after our visit, they demolished the 77-year-old building, and with it, a part of Malaysia that is no longer.

Farther down on Jalan Ampang, we took a circuitous route to find a small road, Lorong Ampang Dua. We located the apartment where the Hoffmans had lived and where we had often stayed and had taken over after they left. The building looked just the same, maybe even in better shape. Further inspection revealed it

15.3 Our former apartment in KL, upper left unit, December 2005

had, rather ironically, become the Russian Centre for Science and Culture, where one could take Russian language lessons—a very difficult endeavor from which Beth and I were taking a break. We dropped in to chat with the deputy director, using a little Russian laced with English and Malay. My Malay was starting to return but not without Russian words interjected!

After a few days in KL, we flew to KK where our son, Derek, then on holiday break from his law studies in Montreal, joined us for the Sabah portion of our trip. Our daughter, Ruth, couldn't come because she was completing her MFA in playwriting in San Diego.

We rented a car and drove from the coast to the park at the base of Mount Kinabalu, 6,122 feet (1,866 meters) above sea level. We spent a few days exploring new developments—a much enlarged hot spring facility, a walkway high up in the jungle's canopy, new restaurants and hotels. This was all too touristic for me—kind of a desecration of the sacred "Lonely Mountain" of my youth. We didn't have the time to climb it, and I don't think my aging "filmmaker's back" could have taken it anyway.

On December 31, we began our descent from the park, but

instead of returning to KK, we turned right on Jalan Ranau Bypass towards Kota Belud. Traveling this road retraced the journeys I had taken almost 40 years earlier on my Norton 500. On a motorcycle, there's much less jostling back and forth. You can lean into the bends of a winding road.

My pulse quickened as we drew nearer Kota Belud. Beth had visited the town only a couple of times in the early 1970s, and this was Derek's first visit, so it was a little difficult to communicate my excitement in visiting a place many still considered to be in the "backwoods." The road's tarmac construction provided places to stop and take photos or to look at the mountain's continually changing faces. I tried, without success, to locate the spot where, on that rainy day in 1969, I had scared a Kadazan farmer over a mud bank and down a steep slope.

As we descended, the road followed a river valley through many small *kampongs*. We entered Kota Belud through the "back door" and rolled down the hill into the center of town to find our hotel, "The Travellers' Lodge." A commercial hotel in Kota Belud seemed incongruent with the town to me. My intrepid former student, Goh Eng Kian, had booked our rooms and he met us there, still the successful organizer and businessman, a solid man of the community.

I could hardly recognize the town center with its whole new blocks of buildings and streets. Hu Hee Bit's restaurant was no more. The whole block of wooden shops had burned down, now resurrected in ugly concrete. I recognized names such as "Ming Soon Trading" and "Wah Sang Hardware" on some shops. Their inventory seemed much the same as it was four decades earlier. People's basic needs had not changed that much.

We drove to my old school and found some classrooms open and empty, due to the holidays. I held a mock teaching session with Goh and my family as students—much more satisfying and humorous than my visit to the school in 1987.

My old bungalow had been practically overgrown with bushes

15.4 Visiting my old bungalow, still standing and occupied

and appeared in great need of paint. I could see curtains in my old bedroom window and a satellite dish on the roof. Goh and I posed for a photo, despite the fact I felt a little depressed about its state.

The house where Caitie had lived was well-preserved in yellow and white paint. I noticed a car, some washing on the line, and children's paraphernalia lying around—great that a family lived there. From this house, we had watched the changing clouds against the mountain and listened to the music of the '60s revolution back home. It remained like a shrine to those times.

Next, we drove to the 10-mile-long Rempayan Beach to take a dip and walk in the rain. Here, long ago, we had raced our motorcycle and swum in the surf, while local fishermen warned us about sharks.

After returning to town, Beth, Derek, and I sat in a *kedai*, drinking tea and watching as people passed by. I tried to describe the meaning of Hu's restaurant to me—the place where I ate most of my meals; learned Malay while bantering with Peter and Hu; watched the circulation of Land Rovers around the town square; and observed the meandering of cattle, goats, dogs, and mad men—and then the rain at four.

That evening, we attended a New Year's party in a Kadazan settlement near Kota Belud. Another former student, Timbon Herbert Lagadan, had invited us. He had been one of my best students. He had earned a B.A. Degree in Theology and then a diploma in planning. At one time, he had been elected to the Sabah State Assembly. At the time of our meeting, he worked as a Political Secretary in the Chief Minister's Department.

At the party, I helped myself to three bowls of fruit bat soup—"good for your health," they told me. We danced to Kadazan gong music. Fortunately, we weren't required to partake in a *tapai* drinking competition. Years before, Beth had become so drunk and sick on this rice beer during a Kadazan harvest festival that she spent most of the evening sleeping it off in one corner of the bamboo floor, oblivious to all.

On New Year's Day, I got up early and went out to take a photo of Mount Kinabalu, the same view that inspired me for the two years I lived in this place. Much to my satisfaction, no highrises or other developments obscured the view.

Next, Goh treated us to a noodle breakfast at his house. Amongst other businesses, he had a noodle shop. Then, in the early afternoon, Goh, Timbon, and twelve more of my former students showed up for a party in a restaurant. Jainisah Nurajim came from KK, now in charge of the Quality Management Unit in the Chief Minister's Department. This seemed appropriate since she had been the most scholastically meticulous of all my students. Jenny Chua also came from KK, as observant and articulate

15.5, 15.6 New Year's Eve at a Kadazan settlement near Kota Belud

15.7 My former students with me, my wife, and son, January 1, 2006

as ever. Others held various posts in government or business. Some faces looked wrinkled and weathered, older than me. Some had already retired, and one had died a few weeks earlier.

I had been right about my predictions when I left Kota Belud back in August 1970. My former students had contributed a lot to Sabah. The general education I helped to impart had made a difference. This small gathering justified every bead of sweat during my two years in the town. The presence of my son on this occasion was like a second layer of icing on the cake they served.

My former students gave me signed copies of *Land Below the Wind* and a picture book on Sabah. After many speeches, toasts, and final goodbyes, we zipped down the new coastal highway. (They told me the old mountain road to KK that I had traveled on by motorcycle had been demoted for use by local traffic only, and was no longer well-maintained.)

We checked into a downtown KK hotel. In the morning, I got up early and went out by myself to a café for my favorite breakfast, *murtabak* and coffee. Then I had one more meeting with a former student who couldn't make it to the New Year's party. This was Datu Tigabelas, "Prince Thirteen." When we met, I could still see the face of the inquisitive student I had known, the one who once asked me the meaning of "to exist," a question which, back in 1968, had made me so excited about my new teaching job. He had passed his Form 5 exams and joined the Kota Belud District Office in 1974. Step-by-step, he had been promoted through the civil service ranks to his present prestigious post as chief protector of Sabah's history, the Director of Sabah's State Archives.

When Mahathir Mohamad became Prime Minister of Malaysia in July 1981, he ordered all government officials to wear tags bearing their names in as short a version as possible. Datu Tigabelas chose "D13." I learned the full story of his name. He was the thirteenth child to be born in his family, but all of his siblings who arrived before him died by the age of four. The doctor at Kota Belud hospital said there was a jinx on the family and to break this, Datu should be named after a number. Datu's father chose "Tigabelas," meaning the number 13, which is not unlucky in East Asian traditions.

Datu's parents had two more children after Datu, but they also died before reaching age four. The number four is unlucky in East Asia because in Chinese, Japanese, and Korean *shi* or *si*, the word for "four," sounds similar to the word for "death." I also learned that Datu had four children, so for protection from "four" and because of his own good luck with "thirteen," he incorporated "Tigabelas" into all of their names.

Datu Tigabelas continued to write articles and deliver speeches on important historical and constitutional matters such as the Philippines' bogus historical claim on Sabah. He made detailed arguments, and I am very proud that I played a part in his training by checking the logic and grammar of his essays when he was a teenager.

When our plane took off from KK airport that afternoon, rising up and over Brunei and the South China Sea, retracing the first route I had taken to Sabah in 1968, I smiled about my own streak of luck in getting to know Sabahans like Datu Tigabelas, Goh Eng Kian, and the others who held the homecoming party for me.

This return to Sabah had been so much better than the one when I was making the film on rattan almost two decades earlier. I had come to learn that everything changes, nothing is static. I call it "flux." If you only attempt to relive your youthful memories, you are doomed to failure. I concluded that there are no absolutes in life. Sometimes, at least for brief periods, you can go home again, and you may be happier for it.

16

No Longer "The Land Below the Wind"

16.1 Marching with my NBFS flag, Madrid, New Mexico, August 1, 2015

ON AUGUST 1, 2015, I marched my newly minted North Borneo Frodo Society flag down the main road of Madrid, New Mexico. A pack of strange-looking people, some in costumes, surrounded me. I had joined the town's second annual "Freak Flag Parade and World's Shortest Pub Crawl." We meandered through the town to the cheers of pub clients, tourists, and residents. About three hundred people live in this former ghost town, once a flourishing mining center. Some settled in the 1960s, and younger people of similar philosophy moved in later.

Maybe labels aren't appropriate, but essentially, Madrid, south of Santa Fe in the New Mexican countryside, is a "hippie town" frozen in time. It has art, craft, and coffee shops, restaurants and pubs, but there's no chain grocery, no commercial pharmacy, and no hardware store. The nearest gas station is seven miles (11.2 km) away. The town does have a volunteer fire department, housed in a building where we gathered before the parade.

How did I get to Madrid? In December 2012, I decided to retire from international work at the end of a large communication project I directed in Washington, D.C. I spent time researching my family's history and visiting my mother and siblings in Elmira, Ontario, a long-day's drive from Maryland. My parents lived long and fruitful lives, continuing to visit Beth and me wherever we lived in Asia and Africa. Shortly after our return from Moscow in 2007, my father died suddenly at age 87. My mother continued to live, somewhat stoically and with failing eyesight, until early 2015, when she passed away at 95 with little fuss—just the way she had lived.

In May 2015, with no real reason to stay on the East Coast, Beth and I decided to put our house up for sale. I wanted mountains, sun, and big blue skies, as in my youth at the University of Calgary where I had received the letter which took me on my life's journey. Online, Beth searched the Albuquerque real estate ads and found an adobe-style house with a pool and room for a studio. We put an offer on it during a quick scouting trip in early June. We returned to pack, sold our Maryland house, and then headed west. Beth attended a calligraphy conference in California, while I took possession of our new house in the Nob Hill neighborhood, two blocks from a preserved section of old Route 66. I made do by setting up camp in the house, sleeping on a foam mattress and eating out in restaurants until Beth returned and our things arrived.

The next order of business was my reactivation of the NBFS. I had seen an ad for the Freak Flag Parade in Madrid on our quick visit in June, and I started to think about this perfect opportunity. I inspected "my precious" NBFS file, which I guarded like Gollum guarded "The One Ring." I had brought it along with me in the car instead of shipping it with our belongings. I selected the organization's crest and map of Middle-Earth superimposed on North Borneo, and took these artifacts to a willing print shop. In just two days, they produced a fine-looking flag, which I mounted on a wooden frame. It was a bit heavy to carry but quite impressive.

That day, my fellow marchers in Madrid had questions about North Borneo, but there was no question about my belonging. I told them, in succinct terms, about the history of the NBFS. Not only had J. R. R. Tolkien become a member of our society, our fame had spread. When I first joined Johns Hopkins in 2001, I met a colleague who had been posted to Sabah with the Peace Corps in the late-70s, long after I had left. We traded stories and he told me an urban legend about Tolkien teaching in Sabah when he was a young man. He said that Tolkien must have returned to start a Frodo Society there. I let him go on for a while before I broke into laughter and told him the true story.

The parade and pub crawl were all consuming, so I slept in a Madrid guest house that night. In the morning, I went directly to the Java Junction for breakfast, where I was immediately identified as "The Man from Borneo." (They didn't say "wild man..." since many people in the town appeared to be a bit "mad," like me, and my declarations were in keeping with the spirit of the place.)

This had been the best of all possible welcomes to New Mexico, a land with a richly diverse population—Native Americans, Hispanos, Hispanics, Latinos, African Americans, recent immigrants from everywhere, as well as a white "Anglo" population, who are not the majority. I liked my new identity as the recently arrived Canadian man from Borneo living in the American Southwest.

Feeling blessed with my re-christening, I drove back to Albuquerque to settle in. Immediately to the east of our desert city at 5,500 feet (1,676 meters) above sea level, the Sandia Mountains majestically rise another 5,000 feet, providing me with a daily reminder of my years under the spell of Mount Kinabalu. In Albuquerque, every day I take a walk to see the ever-changing cloud and light formations on the Sandias, just as I had seen on Mount Kinabalu in Kota Belud.

I felt the need to create and raise my new NBFS flag because on June 5, 2015, a 6.0 magnitude earthquake hit North Borneo with an epicenter near Mount Kinabalu. The quake caused massive landslides, killing eighteen climbers from Singapore, China, Japan, and Malaysia, including four guides. Almost two hundred climbers from various countries were affected. Many were stranded on the mountain but later rescued.

People throughout Sabah, Brunei, and parts of Sarawak felt the tremors and passed along the details, although exaggerated in transmission. The quake damaged many buildings in adjacent districts, an effect which could be expected, given the magnitude. Other more spectacular events occurred. One of the "Donkey's Ears" formations on the summit broke off, and the waters of Poring Hot Spring at the mountain's base turned black.

Some local Kadazan-Dusun natives claimed the cause of the earthquake was the awakening of *aki*, spirits angered by the desecration of Mount Kinabalu by thoughtless Western climbers from Canada, Germany, the Netherlands, and Britain, who had stripped naked and urinated on the sacred summit. Their behavior led to calls for *sogit*, a form of compensation paid in money or livestock, as determined in a trial by Kadazan-Dusun traditional native court. This alone would appease the *aki* and the community, they claimed. But the authorities released the presumed-guilty people, who managed to avoid punishment, probably to protect Sabah's tourist industry. The villagers had to pay for their own cleansing rituals.

I emailed a few of my former students, but no one replied to the few addresses I still had. Perhaps retired and not on email any longer? Tropical climate taken its toll? I could have tried the few phone numbers I still had, but long-distance calls out of the blue can be intrusive and sometimes upsetting.

I searched for the telephone number of Peter, the American Peace Corps guy I lived with in Kota Belud. The number I had for him was out of date. An Internet search turned up some alternatives, so I called and left two voice mail messages. That was all I could do.

I went to *Google* maps on my computer and punched in "Kota Belud, Sabah, Malaysia," clicked "Satellite" and zoomed in. So easy. On "street view," the images of my former North Borneo hometown had been taken on a day in June 2015. Was it before the earthquake? No way of telling. I started by searching for my little bungalow, halfway up the hill overlooking the town. All I could see was a mass of vines under some tall trees. My house had disappeared.

With my cursor, I leapt up the road and around the corner to view the government secondary school where I taught. I was stumped. Too many new buildings and roads, so I zoomed out to find it from above. There it was, now tripled in size. I zoomed back to earth but couldn't find a *Google* street view.

Frustrated, I made a sudden leap back to the Post Office, still in the same location but now housed in a new building with a red-tiled roof. It had been my connection with family and friends in Canada during my two years in Kota Belud: routine airmail letters; a few cables on births, marriages, and deaths; and a couple of prearranged telephone calls.

I took my cursor down the road and through the streets of

the town center, trying to find something familiar. I noticed a shop name I knew, "Ming Soon Trading," located not far from the mosque which had been transformed into a grander affair with three minarets, a bulbous golden dome, and many small towers supporting crescent moons. Down the street from the mosque, I spotted a plastic likeness of Colonel Sanders of Kentucky Fried Chicken fame, smiling at everyone and everything, as if satisfied that he had won a global cultural war.

I left the congested town center and continued on the old road to the capital. I found the Chinese school to the left, now a much larger and imposing building. Down the road to the right, I searched for the Sings' house, where I had spent so many happy hours. They taught me the meaning of acceptance and generosity. The house had disappeared, replaced by some unimpressive office building.

Google maps didn't allow me to climb the small hill across the road, still the home of the Muslim cemetery. Here, in December 1968, we had buried Anderson, our headmaster from Australia. I wondered if the locals remembered him and told stories about his *hantu*, still floating about.

I could have continued down the road, pretending to be on my old motorcycle, trying to find traces of the places I visited, the friends I knew and loved. Or I could have zoomed back through town and out along the north road, passing the long beach on the South China Sea where we avoided sharks and pirates, real or imagined. I could have stayed online indefinitely, searching, comparing, and contrasting these images with my memories, but somehow it seemed all too empty. This virtual journey had become tiring and disappointing.

I thought about the earthquake and wondered if the *aki* had been angered by more than the sacrilegious acts of foreigners. They may have been even more disturbed about the rapid extraction of Sabah's tropical rain forest and the environmental destruction that so-called "progress" had brought. I switched my search on the Internet to get factual updates. I found that Sabah is still an adventure travel destination for bird lovers, jungle hikers, and mountain climbers, but I discovered other, quite disturbing, facts. Its culture had changed.

When I first arrived in Sabah in 1968, the Kadazan-Dusun represented about 30 percent of the population and the Chinese at least 20 percent. Today, these percentages have greatly declined and the largest group has become Filipino Muslims, nearly a million new residents,[1] some who use Sabah as a base for crimes, such as dealing in drugs and smuggling. I discovered that in Sabah, about 58 percent of prison inmates are foreigners, the majority Filipino in origin.[2]

I read that the waters surrounding Borneo are becoming the new hotbed for piracy in the world, surpassing the dangers in the Indian Ocean off the Horn of Africa. I found a year 2000 report about the Abu Sayyaf militant group, aligned with Al Qaeda, invading a Sabahan resort island off the East Coast. I also read stories on how the Chinese were enlarging small islands in the South China Sea to build military bases, only a few hundred miles from Sabah's coastline.

I concluded that Sabah is no longer the "land below the wind" of political tension and conflict. I shut down my computer and closed my eyes, trying to visualize the North Borneo I once knew, a verdant land of tropical rainforest populated with the wild elephants and rhinos of my childhood dreams.

I pulled out an old photo album and flipped it open to study the faded pictures. I had not perused them for many years. Familiar faces and scenes jumped out at me. I also found my old notes, a box of letters my mother returned to me before she died, and a bundle of carbon copies of long-forgotten letters I had written to friends when I lived in Kota Belud. I found amazingly detailed accounts of my first two years in Sabah. All these made up for the diary I never kept. I slid down into my studio chair and began to inspect these artifacts. Other images rushed back from the far corners of my memory as I began to alternate between the letters and the album, cross-referencing like a dedicated archivist.

One photo showed our secondary school, newly opened the week of my arrival—neat red-brick blocks of classrooms with corrugated gray roofs. I inspected other photos of Bajau, Kadazan, and Chinese students—eager and attentive boys and girls, ages 12 to 18. I recalled my challenge in recognizing over a hundred new faces and remembering their names: Dahulim Molonday, Adnan bin Abdul Razak, Wong Chau Soon. I tried to match the faces and names with the photos I took and signatures in the two books they gave me on my last visit to Kota Belud on New Year's 2006. But it was difficult. Their faces had aged too much, and my memory for such detail had faded.

I examined my students' school uniforms in the old photos: dark-blue shorts and skirts with white tops—an effort to minimize ethnic identities and family income differences—although I recalled that some uniforms were well-worn or even tattered. In the photos, the girls are carrying handkerchiefs in their hands, which they used to partially hide their teeth and lips while laughing or talking, a Victorian-like sign of modesty. Or did they use these hankies for secret communication codes that I could never figure out?

As I turned a page of my album, my cell phone rang and I found myself listening to a familiar voice from the past. It was Peter's wife, Arlene. I detected an unusual tone in her opening greeting and I anticipated the news that followed:

"Neill, Peter died three years ago. I tried to contact you but couldn't find your address or phone number."

I fell silent as she described the last years of the man I once knew. He had developed Alzheimer's in his mid-60s. I found it hard to reconcile her words with the mental gymnast I had known, so full of ideas, words, languages, and connections. When I did react, my words sounded like platitudes to me. She gave a little laugh and then told me that she was living with her memories of him every day. We promised to talk again and hung up.

Blessed with my memories of Peter and my sojourns in Sabah, I began to write.

Postscript: A Brief History of North Borneo

KNOWLEDGE ABOUT BORNEO ISLAND has recently increased in importance because of violent conflicts in the area. In the May 2000 attack by the Abu Sayyaf militant group from the Southern Philippines, the insurgents kidnapped twenty-one people—ten tourists, resort workers, and a policeman—and demanded a ransom.[1] The authorities gradually rescued the hostages, but not before they experienced harsh treatment in the jungles of the Philippines. The police and army eventually tracked down most of the kidnappers and killed or jailed them.

In 2013, armed men, supposedly sent by Jamalul Kiram III, a claimant to the throne of the former Sultanate of Sulu, raided the village of Tanduo in Lahad Datu District. The standoff between this group and Malaysian security forces escalated into a full-scale battle, with fifty-six of the self-proclaimed Sultan's followers killed. Others were either captured or escaped. At least ten Malaysian armed forces and civilians died.[2] The attacks continued, including a 2014 strike on a diving resort at Mabul Island, where a policeman was killed and one person kidnapped.[3]

Even more unsettling is the recent conflict in the South China Sea, which forms Borneo's northern shore. It has become one of the most politically precarious places in the world today. This is due to the long-standing claim and recent actions by the People's Republic of China to consolidate its hold over almost all of the sea's waters, islands, shoals, and seabed. Parts of the sea are claimed by Vietnam, a traditional enemy of China; Taiwan, considered only a province by the People's Republic; and by Malaysia, Brunei, and the Philippines.

China's official map, first produced by the Republic of China in 1947 and reproduced by the People's Republic in 1949, includes a broken, nine-dash line in the shape of a cow's tongue that licks up almost all the maritime territory to within 200 miles (322 km) of the coast of these territorial rivals. All these nations also claim mineral, oil, and gas rights over various portions of the sea, as well as its island and shoals. The bed of the South China Sea has proven oil reserves of seven billion barrels and an estimated 900 trillion cubic feet of natural gas.

The International Court of Justice ruled against China's claim on July 12, 2016. But such claims and counter-claims will most likely continue into the foreseeable future. In December 2016, American military intelligence discovered China had established anti-aircraft and anti-missile systems on the artificial islands they constructed. The potential for conflict builds, like festering sores on an untreated patient. The future of this strategic sea has become profoundly uncertain.

Although it is the third largest island in the world, Borneo remains an unknown, mysterious place to many. Most people couldn't find it on a globe without searching. Human skulls 40,000 years old were found over 60 years ago in the Niah Caves of Sarawak, East Malaysia. It was always assumed that these early inhabitants were related to the aboriginal groups of Australia and that they had died out and been replaced by more recent migrants from mainland Asia, around 3,000 years ago. However, researchers have provided evidence recently that these skulls are related to present-day indigenous Bornean groups such as the Iban.[4]

Whatever future research reveals, it is presently believed that these Austronesians—the Iban, Dayak, Kayan, and Penan of present day Sarawak, as well as the Kadazan-Dusun and Murut of Sabah—have inhabited the island for thousands of years. However, the Brunei Malay, Sama-Bajau, Iranun, and Suluk descended from seafarers who, it is estimated, settled along Borneo's coast during the last few hundred years—a migratory process that continues today.

Borneo was once the seat of the Bruneian Empire, a vassal state of Hindu and Buddhist Javanese rulers. The Bruneian Empire expanded throughout the coastal areas of Borneo and western Philippines. Archeologists have found traces of early Chinese trading settlements in many places along the coasts. According to ancient Chinese records, the Bruneian Empire, which the Chinese called Po-ni,[5] was founded in the seventh century. Its rulers and subjects converted to Islam in the fifteenth century due to the influence of Malay- and Arabic-speaking traders, teachers, and missionaries.

The tomb of one ruler of Brunei during the fifteenth century, Maharaja Karna (or Ka-la), whose official Muslim title was "Sultan Abdul Majid Hassan," is located near Nanjing, China. One theory is that he unexpectedly died there, while paying tribute to the Chinese Emperor, after switching allegiance from the Javanese kingdom.[6]

In 1521, after natives of the Philippines killed the Portuguese explorer Ferdinand Magellan, Juan Sebastian Elcano took command of his ship and stopped at Brunei before heading into the Indian Ocean to complete the first circumnavigation of the globe in 1522. Antonio Pigafretta, a scholar on the voyage, reported that Brunei's army had many cannons, and that elephants marched in the Sultan's parades.[7]

The non-exclusive focus of this book is on North Borneo, the northeast corner, which only comprises 10 percent of the island's land mass. In the late 1600s, the Sultan of Brunei ceded the eastern part of North Borneo to the Sultan of Sulu for help in putting down a rebellion. In 1865, the honorary American consul to Brunei, Charles Lee Moses, negotiated with the Sultan of Brunei to gain a 10-year lease to establish a colony called "Ellena," which was to be centered around the Kimanis River and to extend up the West Coast, as far as the Sulu Archipelago. He brought in American and Chinese investors for funding, and Chinese laborers from Hong Kong. But the colony faltered. The British were hostile to this attempt at settlement, and the American government was not interested in investing in the development of the area, due to America's preoccupation with reconstruction following the Civil War.[8]

Next, the rights went to Austro-Hungarian investors who found financial backing from British entrepreneurs. Then, due to inaction, the Sultan of Sulu either ceded or leased North Borneo (depending on differing translations of the Malay word *pajak)* directly to these British investors. Hedging their bets, the British also obtained sovereign and territorial rights for North Borneo from the Sultan of Brunei. They formed the British North Borneo Chartered Company in 1882.[9] As in India, creating a profit-making enterprise was Britain's preferred "hands off" method of colonization. (Had the natives of North Borneo been aware of all this trading and dealmaking over their land, they probably would have been somewhat mystified, if not totally dumbfounded.)

The Company remained in charge until the Japanese invaded Borneo in 1942. After Japan's defeat in 1945, North Borneo became a full British colony until it joined with Malaya, Sarawak, and Singapore to form Malaysia in 1963. (Singapore opted out in 1965.) Also, in 1963, North Borneo reverted to its former name, "Sabah," which was used during Bruneian Empire times. "Sabah" means "morning" or "sunrise" in Arabic.

I can picture the first Muslim traders stepping onto the shore one morning over 500 years ago to see the sun rising over Borneo's northern coast. That's also how I saw it when I first arrived in Sabah in August 1968, a verdant land of glorious morning sunshine, clean air, and flowers.

Illustrations

Chapter Notes

Chapter One

1. Keith, *Agnes Newton. Land Below the Wind,* (Boston, Mass: Little Brown, 1939).
2. Bogdan, Roger. *Freak Show: Presenting Human Oddities for Amusement and Profit,* (Chicago: University of Chicago Press, 1988), 121-127.
3. *The Wild Man of Borneo,* directed by Robert B. Sinclair (Metro-Goldwyn-Mayer, Los Angeles, CA, 1941).

Chapter Two

1. Zubi, Teresa. "Wallacea." Starfish. Archived from the original on 25 May 2017. Accessed on October 14, 2017 at https://www.starfish.ch/dive/Wallacea.html, A synthesis of Wallace, A. R. "On the Zoological Geography of the Malay Archipelago," *Journal of the Proceedings of the Linnean Society: Zoology* no. 4 (1860), 173-178.
2. Rutter, Owen. *British North Borneo: An Account of Its History, Resources, and Native Tribes,* (London: Constable & Company, Ltd., 1922), 11-12. Accessed June 21, 2017 at https://archive.org/details/cu31924023151933
3. Ibid 85.
4. Ling, Alex. *Golden Dreams of Borneo,* (Bloomington, Indiana: Xlibris, 2013), xxii.

Chapter Four

1. Tolkien, J. R. R. *The Lord of the Rings: Part One: The Fellowship of the Rings; Part Two: The Two Towers; Part Three: The Return of the King,* (London: Allen & Unwin, 1966). Reprint by Methuen Publications. Toronto, 1971.
2. Tolkien, J. R. R. Map of Middle-Earth. Accessed July 27, 2017 at http://www.theonering.com/galleries/maps-calendars-genealogies/maps-calendars-genealogies/map-of-middle-earth-j-r-r-tolkien
3. "Oily Man Scare Hits Kota Belud," *The Sabah Times,* Wangsa News Service, Wednesday, March 12, 1969.
4. Rutter, Owen. *British North Borneo: An Account of Its History, Resources, and Native Tribes,* 57.
5. Tolkien, J. R. R. *The Hobbit,* (Boston, New York: Mariner Books edition, 2012), 198-225.

6. Ibid 226-233.
7. Sale, Jonathan. "Ring Three Times," *Punch*, (London: July 25, 1973), 121.
8. Carpanter, Humphrey. *J. R. R Tolkien, A Bibliography*, (London: Allen and Unwin, Ltd., 1977), 230.

Chapter Five

1. Rutter, Owen. *British North Borneo: An Account of Its History, Resources, and Native Tribes*, 28-30.
2. Bidder, Christy, Silverina A. Kibat, and Sairah Saien. "Mount Kinabalu: the Sacred Emblem of the First UNESCO World Heritage Site on Borneo." Accessed October 13, 2017 at http://www.academia. edu/14063923/Mount_Kinabalu_the_Sacred_ Emblem_ of_the_ First_UNESCO_WorldHeritage_Site_on_Borneo

Chapter Seven

1. Association of Diplomatic Studies and Training (ADST), Arlington, Virginia. "A Black Day for Malaysia." Accessed October 13, 2017 at http:// adst.org/ 2016/03/a-black-day-for-malaysia/

Chapter Eight

1. NASA. Spacelog, Apollo 11, Spoken on July 20, 1969, 12:49 p.m. Accessed November 9, 2017 at http://apollo11.spacelog. org/03:23:17:28/#log-line-343048
2. Payne, Robert, *The White Rajahs of Sarawak*, (London: Endeavour Press Ltd., 2016).
3. "Early History of Sibu." Way Back Machine. Accessed October 13, 2017 at https://web.archive.org/web/20150206164730/http://www.thelex. com/sibu/history.html

Chapter Nine

1. Cribb, Robert, "The Indonesian Genocide of 1965-1966." In *Teaching about Genocide: Approaches and Resources*. Edited by Samuel Totten. (Charlotte, North Carolina: Information Age Publishing, 2003), 133-143.
2. *The Look of Silence*, directed by Joshua Oppenheimer (A Final Cut for Real Film, Denmark, 2014). Accessed on Netflix.
3. Jones, Mathew. "Conflict and Confrontation in South East Asia, 1961-1965: Britain, the United States, Indonesia and the Creation of Malaysia," (UK: Cambridge: Cambridge University Press, 2002). Accessed July 21, 2017 at http://assets.cambridge.org/052180/1117/sample/0521801117ws. pdf

4. UNESCO, "Borobudur Temple Compounds," UNESCO World Heritage Centre. Accessed October 17, 208 at http://whc.unesco.org/en/list/592

5. Hanna, Willard A. and Tim Hannigan, *A Brief History of Bali*. (Clarendon, Vermont: Tuttle Publishing, 2016).

Chapter Fourteen

1. Warren, James F. *The Sulu Zone, 1768-1898: Dynamics of External Trade, Slavery, and Ethnicity in the Transformation of a Southeast Asian Maritime State*, (Singapore: National University of Singapore Press, 1981), 114-122.

2. "1985 Lahad Datu Ambush," on Wikipedia. Accessed November 10, 2017 at https://en.wikipedia.org/wiki/1985_Lahad_Datu_ambush

Chapter Sixteen

1. Department of Statistics, Malaysia. Total Population by Ethnic Group, Administrative District and State, 2010. Accessed October 17, 2017 at https://en.wikipedia.org/wiki/Demographics_of_Sabah

2. "Foreigners Make up 58 percent of Sabah Prison Inmates," *The Star*, Bernama News Agency. March 19, 2015. Accessed October 13, 2017 at https://www.thestar.com.my/news/nation/2015/03/19/sabah-inmates-58p-foreign/

Postscript

1. "Twenty Kidnapped from Malaysia Resort Island," *The New York Times*, by Thomas Fuller and the *International Herald Tribune*, April 25, 2000. Accessed November 9, 2017 at http://www.nytimes.com/2000/04/25/news/20-kidnapped-from-malaysian-resort-island.html

2. The Southeast Asia Regional Centre for Counter-Terrorism (SEARCCT), Ministry of Foreign Affairs, Malaysia. Kuala Lumpur, 2016. Accessed November 9, 2017 at: http://www.searcct.gov.my/images/Articles_2016/Bk_Lahad-Datu_2507_NEW.pdf

3. "Gunmen attack diving resort on Malaysia's Borneo Island," *The Telegram*. by APF, July 13, 2014. Accessed July 17, 2017 at http://www.telegraph.co.uk/news/worldnews/asia/malaysia/10964604/Gunmen-attack-diving-resort-on-Malaysias-Borneo-island.html

4. Curnoe, Darren et al. "Deep Skull from Niah Cave and the Pleistocene Peopling of Southeast Asia," Frontiers in Ecology and Evolution, 27 June 2016. Summary accessed October 13, 2017 at https://www.sciencedaily.com/releases/2016/06/160627094831.htm

5. Ling, Alex. *Golden Dreams of Borneo*, (Bloomington, Indiana: Xlibris, 2013), xxii.

6. Rutter, Owen. *British North Borneo: An Account of Its History, Resources, and Native Tribes*, 85.

7. Ibid 86-87.

8. Tatu, Frank, "The United States Consul, The Yankee Raja, Ellena and the Constitution: A Historical Vignette." Persée: Parcourir Les Collections, Vol. 40, No. 1, 79-90, October 13, 1990. Accessed October 13, 2017 at http://www.persee.fr/doc/arch_0044-8613_1990_num_40_1_2667

9. Rutter, Owen. *British North Borneo: An Account of Its History, Resources, and Native Tribes*, 115-148.

Works Cited

Association of Diplomatic Studies and Training (ADST), Arlington, Virginia. "A Black Day for Malaysia." Accessed October 13, 2017. http://adst.org/2016/03/a-black-day-for-malaysia/.

Bidder, Christy, Silverina A. Kibat, and Sairah Saien. "Mount Kinabalu: the Sacred Emblem of the First UNESCO World Heritage Site on Borneo." Accessed October 13, 2017 at http://www.academia.edu/14063923/Mount_Kinabalu_the_Sacred_Emblem_of_the_First_UNESCO_WorldHeritage_Site_on_Borneo.

Bogdan, Roger. *Freak Show: Presenting Human Oddities for Amusement and Profit,* (Chicago: University of Chicago Press, 1988).

Carpenter, Humphrey. *J. R. R. Tolkien, A Biography,* (London: Allen & Unwin, Ltd., 1977).

Cribb, Robert. "The Indonesian Genocide of 1965-1966." In *Teaching about Genocide: Approaches and Resources,* edited by Samuel Totten, (Charlotte, North Carolina: Information Age Publishing, 2003).

Curnoe, Darren, Ipoi Datan, Paul S. C. Taçon, Charles Leh Moi Ung and Soares et al., 2008, 2016; Bae et al. 2014; Liu et al. 2015. "Deep Skull from Niah Cave and the Pleistocene Peopling of Southeast Asia," Frontiers in Ecology and Evolution, 27 June 2016. Summary accessed October 13, 2017 at https://www.sciencedaily.com/releases/2016/06/160627094831.htm

Department of Statistics, Malaysia. Total Population by Ethnic Group, Administrative District and State. 2010. Accessed October 17, 2017 at https://en.wikipedia.org/wiki/Demographics_of_Sabah

Hanna, Willard A. and Tim Hannigan, *A Brief History of Bali,* (Clarendon, Vermont: Tuttle Publishing, 2016).

Jones, Mathew. "Conflict and Confrontation in South East Asia, 1961-1965: Britain, the United States, Indonesia and the Creation of Malaysia. (UK: Cambridge University Press, 2002). Accessed October 13, 2017 at http://assets.cambridge.org/052180/1117/sample/0521801117ws.pdf

Keith, Agnes Newton. *Land Below the Wind,* (Boston, Mass: Little Brown, 1939).

Ling, Alex. *Golden Dreams of Borneo,* (Bloomington, Indiana: Xlibris, 2013).

The Look of Silence, directed by Joshua Oppenheimer. Denmark: A Final Cut for Real Film, 2014). Accessed on Netflix.

NASA. Spacelog, Apollo 11, Spoken on July 20, 1969, 12:50 p.m. Accessed November 9, 2017 at http://apollo11.spacelog.org/03:23:17:28/#log-line-343048.

The New York Times. "Twenty Kidnapped from Malaysia Resort Island," by Thomas Fuller and the International Herald Tribune, April 25, 2000. Accessed November 9, 2017 at http://www.nytimes.com/2000/04/25/news/20-kidnapped-from-malaysian-resort-island.html

Payne, Robert. *The White Rajahs of Sarawak.* London: Endeavour Press Ltd., 2016.

Rutter, Owen. *British North Borneo: An Account of Its History, Resources, and Native Tribes,* (London: Constable & Company, Ltd., 1922). Accessed June 21, 2017 at https://archive.org/details/cu31924023151933

The Sabah Times. "Oily Man Scare Hits Kota Belud," Wangsa News Service, Wednesday, March 12, 1969.

Sale, Jonathan. "Ring Three Times." *Punch,* London, July 25, 1973, 121.

The Southeast Asia Regional Centre for Counter-Terrorism (SEARCCT), Ministry of Foreign Affairs, Malaysia. Kuala Lumpur, 2016. Accessed November 9, 2017 at http://www.searcct.gov.my/images/Articles_2016/Bk_Lahad-Datu_2507_NEW.pdf

The Star, Bernama News Agency. "Foreigners Make up 58 percent of Sabah Prison Inmates." March 19, 2015. Accessed October 13, 2017 at https://www.thestar.com.my/news/nation/2015/03/19/sabah-inmates-58p-foreign/

Tatu, Frank. "The United States Consul, The Yankee Raja, Ellena and the Constitution: A Historical Vignette." Persée: Parcourir Les Collections, Vol. 40, No. 1 (October 13, 1990): 79-90. Accessed October 13, 2017 at http://www.persee.fr/doc/arch_0044-8613_1990_num_40_1_2667

The Telegram. "Gunmen Attack Diving Resort on Malaysia's Borneo Island." By APF, July 13, 2014. Accessed July 17, 2017 at http://www.telegraph.co.uk/news/worldnews/asia/malaysia/10964604/Gunmen-attack-diving-resort-on-Malaysias-Borneo-island.html.

Tolkien, J. R. R. *The Hobbit,* (Boston, New York: Mariner Books edition, 2012).

Tolkien, J. R. R. *The Lord of the Rings: Part One: The Fellowship of the Rings; Part Two: The Two Towers; Part Three: The Return of the King.* London: Allen & Unwin, 1966. (Reprint by Methuen Publications, Toronto, 1971.)

Tolkien, J. R. R. Map of Middle-Earth. Accessed October 13, 2017 at http://www.theonering.com/galleries/maps-calendars-genealogies/maps-calendars-genealogies/map-of-middle-earth-j-r-r-tolkien

UNESCO. "Borobudur Temple Compounds," UNESCO World Heritage Centre. Accessed October 17, 2017 at http://whc.unesco.org/en/list/592

Warren, James F. *The Sulu Zone, 1768-1898: Dynamics of External Trade, Slavery, and Ethnicity in the Transformation of a Southeast Asian Maritime State,* (Singapore: National University of Singapore Press, 1981).

Way Back Machine Internet Archive, "Early History of Sibu." Accessed October 13, 2017 at https://web.archive.org/web/20150206164730/http://www.thelex.com/sibu/history.html

Wikipedia, "1985 Lahad Datu Ambush." Accessed November 10, 2017 at https://en.wikipedia.org/wiki/1985_Lahad_Datu_ambush

The Wild Man of Borneo, directed by Robert B. Sinclair (Metro-Goldwyn-Mayer, Los Angeles, CA, 1941).

Zubi, Teresa. "Wallacea." Starfish. Archived from the original on 25 May 2017. Accessed October 14, 2017 at https://www.starfish.ch/dive/Wallacea.html. A synthesis of Wallace, A. R. "On the Zoological Geography of the Malay Archipelago," *Journal of the Proceedings of the Linnean Society: Zoology.* no. 4 (1860): 173-78.

Glossary of Malay Words and Expressions Used

Agong – king or ruler, referring to the *Yang di-Pertuan Agong*, the Constitutional Monarch of Malaysia

akan – placed in front of a verb to denote future

Allah! Apa yang saya akan buat sekarang? – Oh God! What will I do now?

amah – a nursemaid or maid

amok – behave in a frenzied, out-of-control, or unrestrained manner

angin – wind

apa – what

asli – original

attap – thatch made from palm leaves or fronds

ayer – water

ayer limau – drink made from lemons or limes

badak – rhinoceros

bah or *lah* – word to express emphasis at end of a sentence, *bah*, frequently used in Sabah

bahasa – language

Bahasa Melayu – Malay language, the formal national language of Malaysia

baju – shirt or blouse

baju kebaya – shapely, traditional skirt and blouse combination

balik – to return

Balik nanti? – Return later?

Balik pukul lapan. – Return at eight.

Balik sekarang? – Return now?

balu – widow

banyak – many or much

banyak lain – very different

bapa – father, an honorific for Straits Chinese

barang – goods or belongings

batu – stone or rock, milestone

bechak – a trishaw in which passengers sat in front

belachan – a paste made of mashed, fermented shrimp, chili, and other spices

bemo – a three-wheel taxi-scooter

Berapa harga satu jam? – What's the cost per hour?

besar – big, large

bin – son of

boleh – can do, able to

buat – to make, made, to do, to form, to prepare, to produce, to cause to exist, be or become, to perform (an action, etc.)

bukan – no, not

Bukan tuan. – Not an important person, not a "big man."

bulan – moon, month

bumiputera – literally, "sons of the soil," indigenous peoples

Che'gu – the short-form honorific
  for *Enche guru*, Mister teacher
chichak – gecko, a small lizard which
  clings to walls and ceilings

datang – to come
Datang rumah. – Come to my house.
delman – a horse-drawn carriage
disana – over there

Enche – Mister
Enche guru – Mister teacher

ganja – marijuana
gila – crazy or insane
guru – teacher

haj or *hajj* – pilgrimage (to Mecca)
haji or *hajji* – honorific for a person
  who has completed a pilgrimage
  to Mecca
halal – denoting or relating to meat
  prepared as prescribed by Muslim
  law
hantu – ghost or spirit of a dead
  person
haram – forbidden under Islamic
  law
Hari Rayat Puasa – holiday
  celebrating the end of Ramadan,
  a month of fasting
harimau – tiger
hutan – jungle or forest

jalan – way, path, road, to walk
jalan-jalan – to walk about, stroll
jamban – toilet, latrine, lavatory,
  water closet

kampong – village, community

kampong ayer – community or houses
  built on piles over water
kedai – shop
kedai makan – restaurant
kedai minim – drinking shop
keling, also spelled *kling* – a person
  of Indian origin who resides
  in Southeast Asian Archipelago,
  especially in Malaysia, Singapore,
  or Indonesia; often used in a
  derogatory way, meaning "black
  person"
kerbau – water buffalo
kicap – soya sauce
kicap tomato – tomato sauce
kopi – coffee
kopi susu – coffee served with
  sweetened condensed milk
kuala – confluence, of rivers
kunci – key

lain – other, different
lalang – a tall, tropical grass
lapan – eight
laut – sea, ocean
lumpur – mud

mahu – to want
Mahu ganja? – Do you want
  marijuana?
Mahu makan. – Want to eat.
makan – to eat
makan angin – literally, "eat the wind,"
  to do nothing, to relax
mana – where, how
Mana boleh sampai bulan? – How can
  anyone reach the moon?
Mana ulu? – Where are the
  backwoods?
masuk – to enter

Mat – a prefix to a name, could connote "mad" or crazy

matahari – sun

mati – dead

Melayu – Malay

minum – to drink

murtabak – a stuffed pancake or pan-fried bread, of Middle East origin, which is also commonly found in Malaysia, Singapore, Brunei, Indonesia, and Thailand

naga – dragon

nanti – later

orang – man or person

Orang Asli – original people or Proto-Malays; Austronesian peoples who arrived in the Malaya Peninsula long before the Malays

Orang Japon potong banyak kepala-kepala. – The Japanese cut off many people's heads.

orang-orang – men or people

orang-orang gila – crazy men

orang putih – white man

padang – large field or open space used for sports or public gatherings

padi – rice crops in the field

pajak – to lease or to cede, to tax

paku – nail

pandai – clever or smart

pandan – screwpine leaf, used to add floral-like flavors to barbequed or steamed dishes

parang – long knife, a Malaysian machete

pergi – to go

Pergi (di) mana? – Go (to) where?

potong – to cut

pugai – magic spell

pukul – (n.) o'clock; (v.) to strike, beat, hit continuously

pukul lapan – nine o'clock

putih – white

Ramadan – the ninth month of the Islamic calendar observed by Muslims worldwide as a month of fasting to commemorate the first revelation of the Quran to Prophet Muhammad

rambutan – a medium-size, red-colored, tropical fruit with soft, hairy tentacles

rendang – a spicy, near-dry, coconut-beef curry

roti – flatbread

rumah – house

rumah sakit – hospital; literally, "house of the sick"

saja – only, just

sakit – sick

sampai – to arrive at, to reach

sarong – a tube or length of fabric, worn wrapped around the body and tucked at the waist or under the armpits, worn by both women and men

satay – a dish consisting of small pieces of meat grilled on a skewer and served with a spiced sauce that typically contains peanuts, often spiked with chili

saya – I or me

Saya che'gu saja. – I'm only a teacher.

Saya mahu membantu saja. – I only want to help you.

Saya tidak tahu. – I don't know.
sekarang – now
sempit – narrow, restrictive
setengah – half, one of two equal parts
setengah-setangah – half and half, mid-way
singa – lion
songkok – an oblong hat worn by some Muslim men
sudah – already, placed in front of a verb indicating past action
Sudah makan. – Already eaten.
susu – milk, woman's breast

tahan – endure, bear, stand up to challenges
tahu – to know
tamu – open air market, bazaar
tamu besar – big market
tapai – a crude beer made by fermenting rice

tidak – don't
Tidak apa. – It doesn't matter. Not to worry.
Tidak mahu. – Don't want it.
tigabelas – thirteen
towkay – businessman or owner of business
tuan – sir, honorific for an important man
Tuan mahu pergi di mana? – Sir, where do you want to go?

ulu – the backwoods, remote area

yang – that, which, who, whom, whose
Yang di-Pertuan Agong – the Constitutional Monarch of Malaysia, a position that rotates among sultans of the states of West Malaysia, who vote on succession

North Borneo Frodo Society

Read about its history in this book.

The North Borneo Frodo Society (NBFS) is devoted to increasing the understanding among all peoples of the world and the people of Sabah, Malaysia (formerly British North Borneo), especially now that the once-peaceful South China Sea to the north of this beautiful land is threatened by militaristic, Mordor-like forces. Our members also include all people and organizations in need of some moments of mystery and comic relief in a too fast-paced and conflicted world.

It all started under the shadow of Sabah's Mount Kinabalu (the "Lonely Mountain"), the highest mountain in Southeast Asia, during the waning months of 1968. It was here that the Society was created after the Founding Fathers, Neill McKee and Peter Ragan, experienced an overpowering revelation. In the small town of Kota Belud (most likely Rivendell), they developed their main theory—North Borneo is really Middle-Earth. People joined their society from all around the world. They carried on their research for the next two years: developing comparative maps, discovering the remains of Mount Doom, uncovering stories of an "oily man" (Gollum) who slinks in shadows on moonlit nights, frightening local residents. They employed a Bajau man to forge small NBFS swords, still used by natives who live in the hills near the mountain. They wrote to J. R. R. Tolkien's publisher and the great author joined and patronized the NBFS.

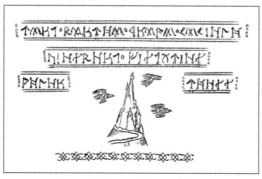

In Frodo We Trust, In Orcs We Disgust!

Visit the NBFS website: NorthBorneoFrodoTolkien.org

About the Author

NEILL MCKEE is a creative nonfiction writer based in Albuquerque, New Mexico. This memoir is about his first overseas adventures in Sabah, Malaysia (North Borneo), where he served as a Canadian volunteer teacher and program administrator during 1968–70 and 1973–74. McKee, who holds a B.A. Degree from the University of Calgary and a Masters in Communication from Florida State University, lived and worked internationally for 45 years and became an expert in communication for social change. He directed and produced a number of award-winning documentary films/videos and multi-media initiatives and authored numerous articles and books on development communication.

Author's website: NeillMcKeeAuthor.com